CULTURAL CONSERVATISM

CULTURAL CONSERVATISM

Toward a New National Agenda

THE INSTITUTE FOR CULTURAL
CONSERVATISM
FREE CONGRESS RESEARCH AND
EDUCATION FOUNDATION

ISBN 0-942522-12-5 (pbk. : alk. paper)

Distributed by arrangement with

UPA, Inc.
4720 Boston Way
Lanham, MD 20706

3 Henrietta Street
London WC2E 8LU England

Contents

Introduction

For much of this century, America's national agenda has been preoccupied with economics. The principal difference between liberals and conservatives has been defined in economic terms. Liberals have been perceived as people concerned primarily with fairness, with seeing that the fruits of prosperity were shared by all segments of society. Conservatives were seen as those concerned mainly with economic freedom and with increasing the common prosperity by spurring economic growth.

These two concerns often seemed to lock our politics into debating the relative merits of Calvin Coolidge and Franklin D. Roosevelt. On the surface, this may still appear to be the case. A Republican administration concerns itself mainly with tax, regulatory, and monetary policies designed to increase the rate of economic growth. The Democratic opposition responds by talking about unemployment, the needs of the less fortunate, and the lagging economic well-being of ethnic minorities.

But beneath the surface, new forces and new ideas have been stirring. Already they have brought about a fundamental shift in electoral politics, as both parties have had to reach out to activist movements built around values, life-styles, and other non-economic issues. Although they are often castigated as "one-issue" interest groups, these movements are in fact the vanguards of a profound political change. The politics that carry us into the twenty-first century will be based not on economics, but on culture.

1

The evidence that this shift of political parameters is already under way is compelling:

• The "regulars" of both political parties have believed for years that the social-issues activists would fade away, lose militancy once their party was in office, or rest content with symbolism. While the activists might need to be appeased in primaries, they could safely be ignored in general elections. These beliefs have proven illusory. The social-issue movements have instead grown stronger in their effects on candidates' positions, on the parties' ability to field campaign workers, on party fund raising (primarily on the Democratic side), and in their ability to provide or withhold a crucial margin of general election victory (especially on the Republican side).[1]

• The Coolidge vs. Roosevelt economic debate is rapidly losing force. The "democratic socialist" model that underlay much of the American left is in disarray all over the world. The intellectual and political pressure which it used to exert against free market institutions has waned greatly. Increasingly, we all advocate free enterprise and respect the marketplace. Our economic debates are losing the apocalyptic character of yesteryear.

• At the same time, other visions of the left remain strong. "National liberation" movements have attracted more than a few Americans to an anti-Western view of world affairs. Radical forms of feminism and environmentalism plus other life-style liberationisms have moved to fill the vacuum left by the collapse of more traditional socialist causes. Thus, as our national debate on economics has moved toward consensus, the debate on values and culture has widened and deepened. A grand synthesis of anti-Western foreign policy with welfare rights, gay rights, and feminist rights threatens to become the next "conscience" of the Democratic party.

• The economic debate itself is being complicated by social and moral issues. As conservatives move to accept a welfare "safety net," its cost rises because of high rates of divorce and illegitimacy.[2] As liberals reach for growth through free enterprise, their flanks are ambushed by calls for "comparable worth."[3]

Meanwhile, both parties are moving to face a situation new in our history: the very real prospect of long-range economic decline. Though it is obscured by bright short-term economic indicators, the underlying situation is that much of our industry no longer competes as effectively as it once did;[4] real living standards have failed to rise in 13 of the last 17 years;[5] and despite a "service economy," many people experience difficulty in getting affordable, high-quality service. While some believe these problems can be solved with conventional remedies—changes in tax policy, business incentives, and trade policy—other observers, both conservative and liberal, see a cultural dimension. As standards decline in personal and professional conduct, businesses ask themselves where they can find a reliable labor force, and workers ask themselves where they can find a competent and honest management.[6]

These factors and others like them are moving us toward a politics centered more, not less, on cultural issues. It is imperative that Americans understand the full significance of this change.

So far, our understanding has been piecemeal and at best partial. We have a vague sense that our culture is adrift and that we live in a time of "changing values." In the activists clustered around the Democratic party, we have tended to see responses to particular "discriminations." In those gravitating to the GOP, we have seen what look like religious "backlashes" against particular affronts to traditional morality.

In fact, both are manifestations of something much deeper. Through several decades of cultural drift, the values, standards, and principles that Americans could count on other Americans to share have been dwindling in number and in content. This process has now brought America to a crossroads of the spirit. The depleted stock of our common ethos must be replenished. But we must choose carefully the nature of the new stock. For this historic and perilous choice, a liberationist left is offering nothing less than a unified agenda of cultural radicalism. The alternative, which has slowly been building in the hearts of a majority of Americans, many of them Democrats, and many of them not notably religious, is cultural conservatism.

What is culture? It is the ways of thinking, living and behaving that define a people and underlie its achievements. It is a nation's collective mind, its sense of right and wrong, the way it perceives reality, and its definition of self. Culture is the morals and habits a mother strives to instill in her children. It is the obligations we acknowledge toward our neighbors, our community, and our government. It is the worker's dedication to craftsmanship and the owner's acceptance of the responsibilities of stewardship. It is the standards we set and enforce for ourselves and for others: our definitions of duty, honor, and character. It is our collective conscience.[7]

The most important component of culture is not "high culture"—the fine arts and masterpieces of literature—but the values to which ordinary people adhere. This is the culture that shapes all of us in our daily lives, in our families, communities, and places of work.

Once we understand what culture is, its importance becomes obvious. Culture is the foundation for everything else. On it depend the economy, civic order, the well-being of families and communities, and, simply, whether things work: whether a nation's products are thoughtfully designed and well made, whether its services function as they should, whether its industry can compete in the world and provide its people with employment, and whether its standard of living and its standing in the world are rising or falling.

Culture's critical role in determining the way a nation functions is often overlooked in debates over politics or economics.[8] Too often, a culture supportive of free institutions or friendly to entrepreneurship is simply presumed, and the success of the society is attributed to a "free market" or "the rule of law." The truth is that without an enterprising people, a free market presides over conspicuous consumption and economic stagnation. Without a culture that roots the law in living habits of restraint, the "rule of law" is a constitutional fiction—a sash across the chest of the colonel who has led the latest *coup*. The post-colonial histories of much of Latin America, Asia, and Africa make the point clearly: a nation's *culture* is what determines its functional success or failure—its ability or inability to provide its citizens with prosperity, opportunities, and personal freedoms.

If this is culture, it is evident that America has been suffering from cultural drift. Cultural drift is the gradual emptying of a nation's values of their content, not by some violent overturning, but by a slow evaporation in which the form is left—in rhetoric and often in manners—but the substance disappears. In America's case, cultural drift has often manifested itself by the replacement of ethical with procedural values. Ethical norms have become more and more a matter of personal preference, while procedural values such as "openness," diversity, pluralism, and the free market (in morals as well as in goods) have taken over the public forum.

Unfortunately, procedural values are not strong enough to bind a nation together. Robbed of substantive standards, schools fall apart, religious denominations lose their influence, parents find their children "out of control," and society dissolves into contending interest groups and increasingly bitter factionalism.[9]

Both liberals and conservatives have been disturbed by America's cultural drift. Both realize that a moral vacuum is dangerous to a nation. The absence of a moral base breeds indifference, a "me first" ethic of greed and ostentation, and a loss of the concept of the common good. Both liberals and conservatives are looking for responses to cultural drift—for revived substantive public values.

Cultural radicalism is one possible response. It is a commitment to refashion the culture of our society to make it conform to certain newly perceived moral imperatives or to certain allegedly scientific (especially psychological or ecological) requirements. Strident demands to eliminate "sexism" and "homophobia" are examples of such moral imperatives. Alleged scientific requirements include the elimination of male aggressiveness as the source of war, the achievement of zero population growth, and the elimination of dogmatic religion as a form of "maladjustment."

Cultural radicalism rejects what might be called "the reality standard," which is a realistic sense of what is achieved or achievable in history. All its demands are unconditional. The historical fact that traditional Western culture has produced societies uniquely free and prosperous counts for nothing. Nor do the historical results of politics based on ruthless purism—the calculated "liquidation" of dissenters and minorities, the concentration camps and gulags, the censorship and thought control, the gas chambers, purges, and killing fields. All of that was yesterday. Today is a new day, and all that counts are pure intentions. No evidence is allowed to contradict the view that Western societies are sinkholes of racism, exploitation, and inhumanity.

All of us can understand the need to reconsider past attitudes, right historic wrongs, or adjust our actions to new discoveries. But how we go about this task is different. Most of us balance new ideas and ideals against the accumulated wisdom of our culture—against common sense. We use our historical and moral inheritance, including our religious faith, as the framework for devising plausible reforms.

Cultural radicals proceed differently. For them, a new insight invalidates the old framework. It exposes all previous existence as an inheritance of oppression or ignorance. The past can serve as no counterweight, and its lessons cannot yield contrary evidence. The new imperative or requirement becomes the core of a new framework, the litmus test of a new humanity.[10]

We encounter cultural radicalism in many settings. On a typical university campus, one need not wander over to the Womens' Studies Department; one can find it as well in the treatment of literature ("deconstruction") or in classes at the law school ("Critical Studies").[11] Off campus, we can find it in the prurient arrogance of a television talk-show host, in the patronizing tone of a "committed" clergyman or social worker, in the disruptive wake of a court order, and (in a different sense) in many a rock video. Most importantly, perhaps, we encounter the effects of this radicalism in its past successes. Major institutions, such as our schools and colleges, have been weakened—and personal morals have been altered—because of the ideas popularized and the "revolutions" proclaimed by cultural radicals in the 1960s.[12]

If this is cultural radicalism, what is cultural conservatism?

Cultural conservatism is the belief that there is a necessary, unbreakable, and causal relationship between traditional Western, Judeo-Christian values, definitions of right and wrong, ways of thinking and ways of living—the parameters of Western culture—and the secular success of Western societies: their prosperity, their liberties, and the opportunities they offer their citizens to lead fulfilling, rewarding lives. If the former are abandoned, the latter will be lost.

Several important beliefs help to define cultural conservatism more fully. First is a belief that traditional values and virtues are required not only to create a society that is free and prosperous, but also for individual fulfillment.[13] Unlike cultural radicalism, virtually all the world's great religions and philosophies have argued that limits on instinctive human behavior are necessary for individuals to live rewarding, satisfying lives. While these limits impose short-term burdens, they are conducive to long-run happiness. In contrast, immediate gratification of instinctive desires leads to long-term self-degradation and dissolution.

Since the 1960s, this traditional view has faced a major political challenge from culturally radical advocates of "liberation." Liberationists see traditional limits on behavior as unnatural restrictions on happiness. They believe that if something is pleasurable and "self-expressive" in the short run, it must contribute to personal growth. They argue that any restrictions on personal behavior violate new-found "rights" of life-style autonomy.[14]

Liberationist views would have garnered little popular

support, were they not amplified politically and seconded by some developments in pop culture. Television in particular has spread the message that happiness rides in the "fast lane." The good life is built not on producing a sound product, personal growth or serving others, but on the acquisition of chic things and intense experiences. Rock music has seduced its youthful audience with provocative messages of "feeling good" and "doing it."

To the cultural conservative, man's whole history argues the opposite case: true happiness is built on self-discipline and moderation. Real personal growth is something called maturity, and it comes from internalizing limits, not denying them.

A second belief underpinning cultural conservatism is that society, including government, must play an active role in upholding traditional culture. The reason is simple: in a cultural "free market," the limits, restraints, and self-disciplines required by traditional ways of living cannot compete with aggressively promoted "liberationisms." Human nature leads most people to put today's pleasure above tomorrow's unless there are immediate costs in doing so—costs in terms of peer pressure, social acceptance, and, in criminal cases, legal sanctions. Indeed, the existence of a criminal code is a pointed reminder that society cannot be neutral: if it takes a "value-free" stand, it smiles impartially upon the victim and the attacker. If society is not value-neutral, it favors somebody's culture. We believe it should favor our traditional culture.

This view of society and government as forces acting in support of traditional values and culture, not as legislative bullies, but with funding and advocacy, distinguishes cultural conservatives from some others who have been grouped with them under the conservative label. It divides them from extreme libertarians, who favor a complete free market of morals.[15] It divides them from some purely economic conservatives, who seem to believe that a growing economy will solve all cultural problems.

A third belief of cultural conservatives returns to the very foundation of our discontent with cultural radicalism. We believe in "taking the long view." In a time when "old" means ten years ago and "the future" means the time between now and the next election, cultural conservatives insist on looking back over the centuries in their search for wisdom and looking ahead to what the actions proposed for tomorrow will mean to our children, their children, and their children's children.

Taking the long view does not mean conferring infallibility on remote ancestors. It means securing full information about a problem. For the long view is also the broad view. The evidence available a century or a millennium back does not become invalid simply because time has passed. While society has changed enormously since the days of Homer or Moses, there is common ground between us and them in the continuity of human nature.

Similarly, cultural conservatives are less concerned whether their measures are expedient now than whether they will serve the generations who come after us. We have a sacred trust to preserve what our fathers built so painfully for us, a society unusually free and prosperous, and to pass it on to future generations.

That trust must be the hallmark of our political agenda. The dwindling stock of our common and public virtues must be replenished, not from untested sources, but from the proven tradition of our civilization.

Cultural conservatism has intellectual roots in Russell Kirk's *The Conservative Mind* (1953) and in the broad reach of his later book, *A Program for Conservatives*. Like Kirk, cultural conservatives deal with a theme not prominent in modern American political thinking and deal with it in a way different from much European thought. Between the French Revolution and World War II, a number of European countries experienced political movements of a religious and cultural cast: they were restorationisms, romantic, clerical, or fascist, and they were almost always disfigured by anti-Semitic bigotry. (In fact, most American Jews are descended from refugees from precisely such a movement in late 19th century Russia.) An American "cultural conservatism" patterned on such movements would merit deep suspicion. It would give rise to legitimate fears on the part of those who felt they might not be "native" enough to pass its "cultural" or sectarian muster.

Let it be understood, therefore, that cultural conservatism as here defined and advocated is not a restorationism. It does not seek to "restore" a pre-modern form of social order, alleged to be sweeter and more agreeable than the industrial hurley-burley of democratic capitalism. Quite the contrary, what we mean by cultural conservatism assumes the basic goodness and applauds the creativity of the modern form of society. We merely note that its rise and continuance depend upon cultural factors which (a) do not exist everywhere and (b) are in danger of being lost among us. The culture we wish to preserve and inculcate has been a cause of the modern order, not a victim of it.

Cultural conservatism has other roots in recent American experience. These roots include the New Right and the Religious Right. The fact that both of these movements have come under heavy attack, especially the Religious Right, should not be allowed to obscure the fact that they have been pioneers in the effort to respond to cultural radicalism. They began the task of reorienting American conservatives from economic issues alone to social and value-related issues. They remain important components of the cultural conservative movement, for the simple reason that any New Right or Religious Right conservative is also, virtually by definition, a cultural conservative.

The Right to Life movement has been another precursor of cultural conservatism. It has drawn public attention to what is perhaps the sharpest conflict between traditional values and cultural radicalism: the conflict between reverence for life and a "new morality" in which life is a secondary consideration. Reverence for the life of the innocent is possibly the most powerful single norm of traditional Western culture. It lies at the heart of long enduring efforts to restrain war, to care for the poor and for children, to provide for the elderly, and to advance public health and medical science. Contempt for life, such as the Nazi's contempt for the lives of six million Jews, has been abhorrent to us.

Cultural radicalism has undermined this most central of traditional values. Abortion on demand is its most prominent victory, but others threaten: infanticide, euthanasia, "termination" of the bed-ridden elderly, approval of suicide and assistance in committing it. Even those who have disagreed with the pro-life movement on public policy should acknowledge that it has opened a vista on a large issue: our right to life in the face of ideologies, circumstances, or vulnerabilities that lead others to seek our deaths.[16]

Cultural conservatism also has roots among those for whom the most basic political issue is the nature of man, and who believe man's nature to be constant.[17] The immutability of human nature, as both a political belief and an anthropological fact, is a staunch bulwark against cultural radicalism's promises of a "new man," unlike previous humanity.

Aspects of cultural conservatism are also to be found outside the existing conservative movement. Millions of largely apolitical Americans have grown suspicious of "new moralities" and other instant causes.[18] They may not be connoisseurs of high culture, but they understand the strengths of the culture we already have. They value the man-from-Missouri perspective it gives us on radical chic and designer ideas. They look to it to rescue us from growing up ignorant of what is worth learning. They know that our traditional culture (and it alone) can rebuild a community of values, in place of mutual contempt, between ordinary citizens and the elites of our society. It alone can bind us to our ancestors and to our posterity.

This same traditional culture includes the liberal mind in the best sense of that term—the largeness of vision, the ability to innovate, the sense of paradox and fruitful tension, the respect for critical reason. The collapse of intellectual standards, especially in the professions, and the demand of culturally radical "orthodoxies" to control thought and speech (a demand quite evident on many campuses) represent far greater threats to the liberal mind than occasional preachers of illiberal views or parents who object to certain textbooks.[19]

In Europe, but also increasingly in the United States, many once-leftist intellectuals are moving away from their radicalism and toward cultural conservatism.[20] They have come to realize that traditional culture is the only effective barrier against totalitarianism. They see that cultural radicals find any autonomy in the cultural order intolerable. Radical censorship does not stop at the political columns of newspapers. Radicals demand control of what novels can be written, what films can be seen, what works of history can be shelved in libraries, what research can be undertaken by scientists, and what segments of reality can be probed by philosophers. They seek to intercept all communication between one generation and the next, until they have formed "new humans" who will conceive of nothing (and pray to nothing) higher than the Reich or the Commune.

This growing awareness of freedom's cultural foundations is leading artists, writers, film-makers, and journalists to begin to celebrate the common ground they share with ordinary citizens and to set aside the fashionable poses of yesteryear, the pleasures of "alienation" and the joys of shocking the "booboisie."

All these movements and groups, and more, contribute to the cultural conservative movement. Cultural conservatism elicits from each of them the conclusion toward which they all tend—some for religious reasons, some for moral, artistic, pragmatic or economic reasons. It is the conclusion that traditional Western culture is demonstrably functional—that it has given rise to supremely successful societies—and that our drift away from it puts at risk everything we have achieved as a people.

Cultural conservatism encourages each of these contributory groups to pursue by its own lights and principles the philosophical and theological questions which go to the roots of our culture. Some will want to validate these roots in absolute terms, as deriving from God. Others will be content to see them as purely secular, a matter of what mankind has learned about itself over many generations. Cultural conservatism does not exclude the agnostic, the atheist, someone who follows a non-Western religion or philosophy, or a person who separates his religion and philosophy from his political beliefs. Such an individual can be as firm a cultural conservative as someone who derives his political philosophy from Judaism or Christianity, provided that he shares the basic insight that traditional values are functional values. The case for cultural conservatism can be made in wholly secular terms.[21]

This focus on traditional culture's secular functions opens cultural conservatism's door to a broad range of people. It permits the formation of a wide coalition of individuals and movements, all of whom see in their own way the need to be active in upholding traditional culture. Agreement on this need defines a cultural conservative, and on this agreement, a majority coalition can be built.

NOTES

1. On the Democratic side, the rising influence of pro-choice and feminist groups is documented by Ethel Klein, *Gender Politics* (Harvard, 1984). On the Republican side, the growing importance of pro-life and evangelical groups is studied by Stuart Rothenberg and Frank Newport, *The Evangelical Voter* (Washington, D.C.: Institute for Government and Politics, Free Congress Research and Education Foundation, 1984).

2. According to the Civil Rights Commission, increasing divorce and unwed motherhood "are responsible for essentially all of the growth in poverty since 1970." The United States Commission on Civil Rights, *A Growing Crisis: Disadvantaged Women and Their Children* (Washington, D.C., 1983), Clearinghouse Publication No. 78.

3. Women's Research and Education Institute of the Congressional Caucus for Women's Issues, *Gender at Work* (Washington, D.C., 1984); Michael Levin, "Comparable Worth: The Feminist Road to Socialism," *Commentary*, September 1984, 13–19.

4. The notion of 'competitiveness' has become so controversial that it is hard to find indicators of its rise or decline on which both sides agree. But it seems safe to cite at least the following:

• our technological lead has evaporated in many areas; in the 1950s, 82% of the major inventions brought to the market were developed in the United States; by 1970 only 55% originated here, and the percentage is still falling, according to the National Science Board *(Science Indicators: The 1985 Report)*;

• between 1960 and 1983, our annual increase in productivity averaged only 1.2%, compared to 3.4% for West Germany and 5.9% for Japan;

• between 1977 and 1986, our overall industrial production rose by about 25%, while Japan's rose over 44%;

• for each thousand workers, 813 days are lost each year in the U.S. because of labor unrest, while only 31 days are lost in Japan, and only six days in Germany

• for at least the last 14 years, the U.S. savings rate has been the lowest in the industrialized world; our gross private savings are no longer sufficient to finance both domestic investment and the net government deficit; the gap has had to be filled with foreign capital.

5. When adjusted for inflation, median family income stayed virtually flat during the entire decade from 1970 to 1980, declined in '81–'82, and has only begun to grow again in the last two years; median household income actually declined more than 4% between 1970 and the mid-1980s.

6. Decline in the "work ethic" has been suspected for a long time but dismissed as a non-measurable factor. Amitai Etzioni, however, has some hard evidence to report. An average automobile worker in Japan turns out 40 to 50 cars per year, compared to 25 in the United States; an average Japanese steelworker turns out 421 tons a year, compared to 250 in our country; see Etzioni, *An Immodest Agenda* (New York: McGraw-Hill, 1983), pp. 232ff. Etzioni also deals with declines in the executives' work ethic, on which Marshall McLuhan has striking things to say *(Take Today: The Executive as Drop-Out)*, as do Robert H. Hayes and William J. Abernathy, "Managing Our Way to Economic Decline," *Harvard Business Review* 58 (July–August, 1980).

Changes in the values that motivate workers have also been charted by the research firm of Yankelovich, Skelly and White;

see "The New Psychological Contrast at Work," *Psychology Today*, May 1978, p. 49.

Still other indicators point to a rising tide of theft, vandalism, alcohol and drug abuse on the job. See "A $40 Billion Crime Wave Swamps American Business," *U.S. News and World Report*, February 21, 1977, p. 47.

7. To most Americans, the word 'culture' no doubt suggests something much narrower in meaning and much more dispensable from the point of view of ordinary people. The word suggests "cultivation" of tastes and manners, perhaps to an artificial or hoity-toity degree. This is not what we mean at all.

Our definition of culture is based on a use of the word which has become standard among anthropologists. See, for example, E. B. Tylor, *Primitive Culture* (London: J. Murray, 1871), p. 1; Alfred Kroeber, *Anthropology* (New York: Harcourt, Brace, Jovanovich, 1948), p. 8; Marvin Harris, *Cultural Materialism: The Struggle for a Science of Culture* (New York: Random House, 1979), p. 47; Ward Goodenough, "Frontiers of Cultural Anthropology: Social Organization," *Proceedings of the American Philosophical Society* 113 (1969), p. 330; Alfred Kroeber and Clyde Kluckhohn, *Culture: A Critical Review of Concepts and Definitions* (Harvard University Press, 1952), p. 181.

Our definition of culture is broad but not vacuously so. Culture still contrasts with the material environment and with the invariable features of human nature. Explanation of long-term historical trends in terms of culture represents a definite alternative to racist theories and to the biological reductionism present in the "trigger" theories proposed by some sociobiologists; it is also an alternative to psychological explanations of the Freudian type.

8. America's Founding Fathers did not commit this oversight. As Robert Nisbet comments, ". . . what was present in very substantial measure in the basic works of the founders of political democracy was respect for such social institutions as property, family, local community, religion, and voluntary association, and for such cultural and social values as objective

reason, the discipline of language, self-restraint, the work ethic, and, far from the least, the culture that had taken root in classical civilization and grown, with rare interruptions, ever since. If we neglect the role of these institutions and these values in the minds of the Founding Fathers, we have omitted the elements on which alone, in their minds, political democracy could be made a reality," *The Twilight of Authority*, pp. 76f.

9. It is often alleged that cultural drift is inevitable in a free society, or is just one of the prices one has to pay for freedom. But as Friedrich Hayek observes, the true mark of a free society is its ability to achieve a measure of self-correction without centralized coercion. "The existence of individuals and groups simultaneously observing partially different rules provides the opportunity for the selection of the more effective ones." A society which must renounce all effort to correct its cultural drift is not free, then, but is a slave to its more destructive tendencies. See Friedrich A. Hayek, *The Constitution of Liberty* (Chicago: University of Chicago Press, 1960), p. 63.

10. For this contrast—reform "inside a framework of both values and institutions which is not of our own making" vs. reform which "synthetically constructs" a new framework—see again Hayek, *loc. cit.*

11. For introductions to these movements, see Colin Campbell, "The Tyranny of the Yale Critics," *New York Times Magazine*, February 9, 1986, pp. 20ff; Jeffery D. Troutt, "Bias, the Law School Dilemma," in Patrick B. McGuigan and Jeffrey P. O'Connell, eds., *The Judges War* (Washington, D.C.: Free Congress Research and Education Foundation, 1987), pp. 193–210.

12. A major sociologist has said, "I think it would be difficult to find a single decade in the history of Western culture when so much barbarism—so much calculated onslaught against culture and convention in any form, and so much sheer degradation of both culture and the individual—passed into print, into music, into art, and onto the American stage as the

decade of the 1960's." Robert Nisbet, "The Nemesis of Authority," *Encounter,* August 1972, p. 17.

13. Hayek agrees in a passage which could hardly be improved: "There probably never has existed a genuine belief in freedom, and there has certainly been no successful attempt to operate a free society, without a genuine reverence for grown institutions, for customs and habits and 'all those securities of liberty which arise from regulation of long prescription and ancient ways,' Paradoxical as it may appear, it is probably true that a successful free society will always in a large measure be a tradition-bound society," *op. cit.,* p. 61. The author whom Hayek is quoting is Joseph Butler.

14. In this respect their ancestor is Jeremy Bentham, who contended that "every law is an evil, for every law is an infraction of liberty." See his *Theory of Legislation* (5th ed., London, 1887), p. 48.

15. Such libertarians part company with Hayek, who declares inherited moral rules to be "a condition of freedom." He discusses culturally inherited rules and concludes as follows: "It is indeed a truth, which all the great apostles of freedom outside the rationalistic school have never tired of emphasizing, that freedom has never worked without deeply ingrained moral beliefs and that coercion can be reduced to a minimum only where individuals can be expected as a rule to conform voluntarily to certain principles." *Op. cit.,* p. 62. In a footnote, Hayek directs the reader to these concurring opinions:

Edmund Burke: "Men are qualified for civil liberty, in exact proportion to their disposition to put moral chains upon their appetites; in proportion as their love of justice is above their rapacity; in proportion as their soundness and sobriety of understanding is above their vanity and presumption; in proportion as they are more disposed to listen to the counsel of the wise and good, in preference to the flattery of knaves," *Letter to a Member of the National Assembly;*

James Madison: "To suppose that any form of government will secure liberty or happiness without any virtue in the

20   CULTURAL CONSERVATISM

people, is a chimerical idea," in debates during the Virginia ratifying convention, June 20, 1788.

16. For the current outlook and program of this movement, see Dave Andrusko, ed., *To Rescue the Future, The Pro-Life Movement in the 1980s* (Toronto: Life Cycle Books, 1983).

17. Those who hold this view against its relativist or historicist critics include not only philosophers like Leo Strauss and his pupils but also biological and social scientists like E. O. Wilson and Marvin Harris.

18. For example, people have turned sharply against the view that homosexual relations should be legalized (Gallup Poll, October 23, 1986); three Americans out of four would allow religious groups and clubs to meet in public school buildings, and a similar majority favors Bible study in public school classes (Gallup Poll, November 23, 1986); people who describe themselves as "very traditional" and "old-fashioned" in their moral views (including matters of sex, family life, and religion) outnumber those who describe themselves as "very liberal" or "modern" by better than three to one; no more than 21% favor the legalization of marijuana, and as few as 4% favor the legalizing of pornography (*Public Opinion,* Nov/Dec 1986, p. 33).

19. People understand this; so after a decade of unpersuasive cries of alarm, with titles like *God's Bullies* and *Thunder on the Right,* Americans have reacted with a real sense of alarm to Allan Bloom's *The Closing of the American Mind.*

20. Aleksandr Solzhenitsyn's works have been most influential in this regard. Christopher Lasch's *Haven in a Heartless World* and *The Cult of Narcissism* have also had a sobering impact.

21. Which does not mean that we consider religion irrelevant. See the section on moral and religious institutions, below.

Policy Areas

How does cultural conservatism approach the task of developing a specific policy agenda?

Cultural conservatives are optimistic about America's long-term future. We believe our basic culture is sound, and that it is still alive in the hearts and minds of most Americans. It is because we are optimists that we think our nation's problems can be faced squarely and conquered.

Our long-range optimism gives us the courage to look objectively at the disturbing pattern of the present. It is a wide-reaching pattern of decay and decline. As more and more marriages dissolve, the general birthrate heads downward, while the rate of pregnancy outside of wedlock turns sharply up.[1] In education, too many high school graduates are functional illiterates,[2] and too many college graduates are cultural illiterates, even when they hold prestigious degrees. We seem to have a dearth of great men in public life, while the private sector abounds in colorless "managers" and Wall Street manipulators. Our manufactured products have trouble competing effectively even in their home market. Personal responsibility has been replaced with endless litigation.

Neither political party seems able to devise national policies that work. We can fund current consumption only through an enormous deficit, which is to say, by taxing future generations. We have become the world's largest international debtor. Our foreign policy seems unable to progress beyond ideas developed in the 1940s. Large increases in defense spending yield little or no growth in military strength. Welfare programs, instead of helping the poor, have created a permanent underclass. Violent crime runs at a rate with no parallel in any other developed country.

There are also some hopeful signs. Some industrial firms are rejecting the rigid, depersonalizing, bureaucratic organizational model that has come to characterize American business and are turning instead to the participatory corporative model. A "return to basics" movement in education is raising reading and mathematics skill levels in many schools, including some in difficult innercity areas.[3] Some colleges have introduced a core curriculum designed to educate, not just train. The military reform movement, driven largely by younger officers, seeks to refocus our armed services away from budgeting, management, and promotion politics and back on the art of war and winning in combat.

In virtually all these cases the key to reform and renewal has been recognition of the cultural origins of the problem—often in the form of institutional culture—and a return to tradition.

Many of our problems are rooted in a fairly recent cultural breakdown among the elite. Most Americans continue to adhere in large measure to our traditional culture, and they find that it works. They know it can again work for the nation as a whole, including the elite—much of which is increasingly disenchanted with the results of "liberation" and materialism.

The task before us is to set a new national agenda that takes a clear-eyed look at our problems, identifies their cultural roots, and moves to resolve them, to reverse our areas of decline and replace them with nothing less than an American renaissance.

It can assuredly be done.

It will require new concepts. Our new agenda must not only offer new answers, but ask new questions. It must not only propose new approaches in existing policy areas, but define new areas and new issues. It must constitute the basis for a new politics.

The agenda offered here is an agenda for governing. Governing requires actions by government. It is not merely a matter of saying, "Get the government out of x or y," or "privatize everything." As cultural conservatives, we believe government, including the Federal government, has legitimate tasks and duties, including not only upholding public order but also promoting the general welfare and the common good.

We also believe government action must be bounded by the concept of limited government. From our heritage as a free people, we derive two limits which have the highest importance. They are subsidiarity (often called federalism) and reliance on mediating institutions.

Subsidiarity is the principle that the more local the level on which a decision can be made and action taken, the better. Society decides and acts on a number of levels: the individual, the family, the local community, the state and the nation, with others interspersed along the way. The more local the level at which a problem can be dealt with or a decision taken and implemented, the more likely it will be to reflect reality, accord with local circumstances, directly involve the people affected, lead to effective action, and preserve that most important of liberties, liberty in the way we live our daily lives. To this end, subsidiarity dictates that a higher level of authority—especially the Federal government—should only intervene in the business of more local levels under extraordinary circumstances. Further, the purpose of the intervention must be to repair the lower level and then get back out, letting it resume its proper functions. The higher level should never take over on a permanent basis. Unfortunately, this principle is widely flouted in the United States. The Federal government, once it intervenes, tends to take over permanently. For the sort of initiatives proposed in this agenda to work, there will have to be an ironclad commitment on the part of Federal authorities to reverse their unwarranted permanent interventionism.

Mediating institutions stand between the individual citizen and government, and thereby prevent the reduction of society to lone individuals facing an immensely powerful, all-pervasive state apparatus. They reflect subsidiarity, and can only exist where all levels of government respect it. The most important mediating institution is the family. Others include churches, professional associations, labor unions, businesses, service organizations, and a free press.

In a healthy society, many public problems are dealt with by mediating institutions rather than government. They are often much more effective, because they can be more personal, adapting to individual needs; because the volunteer efforts they depend on often bring a higher level of commitment than professional services provide; and because they minimize burdensome rules, regulations and red tape. Cultural conservatives believe government at all levels should cherish mediating institutions, letting them do all they can and encouraging them in their missions.

As cultural conservatives, we generally prefer the free market to government action. We prefer it not because of some ideology, but because the market is generally more effective in meeting needs. But sometimes government action is necessary. For example, the market for toxic wastes being limited, it is probable that government will need to help clean them up. Where the free market is irrelevant, ineffective, or excessively cruel, government—but preferably local government—has a proper and necessary role.

We also recognize that individual economic liberty is only possible in a society where conventions are respected (the current litigation explosion is in part a product of the breakdown of conventions and civility), where change occurs organically rather than by ideological *fiat,* and where a sense of community, especially a community of values, is fostered. Government must be active in securing the preconditions for economic freedom.

Within this limiting framework, the agenda offered here reflects a certain governmental activism. In fact, it seeks to revive one of the central tenets of President Roosevelt's New Deal: experimentalism. In each area, it attempts to be clear and firm about goals, and yet tentative and highly experimental as to means.

The reason for experimentalism is simple: people are not predictable. It is not possible to know in advance whether a program will bring its intended result. As the past forty years have shown, programs can bring results quite the opposite of what was intended.[4] We must be willing to question and test the effectiveness of all programs, and to terminate them when they are ineffective. When that happens, the rule must be: try something else. If means become ends, everyone suffers. Flexibility as to means, willingness to experiment, to admit failure and try a different approach must characterize any agenda, especially one that has a new and very different starting point, as does the agenda proposed here.

The governmental activism proposed here would seldom take the form of legislation or massive spending. Most often, it would be leading by example and using the government's "bully pulpit" to point out the virtues of our cultural traditions—and the effects of our lapses from them. Leading by example can be especially effective. After all, if we want to re-create a society where things work, what better place to start than in our government departments?

In the cases where Federal legislation is proposed in this agenda, it generally relates either to reform of the Federal government itself—e.g., reforming Federal court procedures to focus them on determining guilt or innocence—or to empowerment. Empowerment—providing people the means with which they can solve their own problems—is a long-standing and legitimate activity of the Federal government. As conservative market-theorist Michael Novak writes:

> The people of the United States in establishing their government, as stated explicitly in the Preamble to the Constitution, did so in order to "ensure justice" and "promote the general welfare." There are some things that government can legitimately do to promote the achievement of the common good in many dynamic ways that are consistent with, but go beyond, concerns for mere "public order." And it can do these things without infringing upon liberties, without ceasing to base its actions upon the "consent of the governed," and without transgressing the bounds of limited government. Among such people-empowering actions by our own government might be cited the Homestead Act, the land-grant colleges, the Highway Act, rural electrification, the Social Security Act, food stamps, housing assistance, AFDC, and a host of others.[5]

The challenge is to devise ways to undertake empowering actions without generating Federal bureaucracies to "manage" the resulting programs. Liberals and con-

servatives increasingly agree that bureaucracy is a problem, not a solution. Almost without exception, bureaucracies (government and private) serve not their intended
purposes, but themselves. Their primary goals are self-
perpetuation and self-aggrandizement: expanding their
size, budget, power and perquisites, and sometimes actually perpetuating the problem they were established to
solve in order to perpetuate themselves.

How can government act without acting through bureaucracies? We offer a few possible answers here. In
the section on institutional design, we suggest the con-
version of Federal departments from the bureaucratic to
the corporative model. In the section on welfare, we
propose expanded use of mediating institutions in the
delivery of benefits. When we turn to the environment,
we suggest using government resources to establish
trusts, such as a Wilderness Trust, that would be man-
aged by people who had previously been active in a
relevant field on a private, non-profit basis.

We make repeated use of revolving funds. The general
idea of a revolving fund is that the government money
put into it is loaned out and then paid back by the
beneficiaries of the loans, so that the fund is restocked
for the next round of beneficiaries. In our proposals the
funds have some special anti-bureaucratic features. Let
us say the Federal government decides to establish a
program in policy area x. The program would permit—
not compel—states to establish revolving funds that
would further the program's aims. If a state decided to
participate in the program, the Federal government
would cede certain Federal taxation rights to the state
for the purpose of funding the state's initial contribution
to the fund. Because the whole idea of a revolving fund
is that it is self-sustaining, once the state's initial contribution had been funded, the ceded taxation rights would

revert to the Federal government. If the state wanted to make further contributions to the fund, it could do so, but it would have to pay for it out of the state's own budget. To ensure that the Federal program's purposes were served, the taxation rights would only be ceded for the specific purposes of the program. A state could not ask for the taxation rights for any other purpose.

An example may help to make this more clear. Let us say the Federal government decided it wanted to promote family businesses among the poor. It would establish a program under which states could choose to set up a venture capital revolving fund for family businesses. Let us assume Pennsylvania decides to do so. The Federal government, under the program, would provide Pennsylvania money up to a certain total—say, $100 million—to establish the revolving fund. It would provide the $100 million not through a direct grant, which tends to bring Federal bureaucratic controls, but by ceding to Pennsylvania Federal taxation rights on, say, alcohol. Once Pennsylvania had taken in the $100 million from the ceded alcohol tax rights, those rights would revert to the Federal government. It would be Pennsylvania's responsibility to see that the fund really revolved: to ensure that money paid out from it was returned. Pennsylvania could choose to put more of its own money into the fund, either to expand it or to keep it going in the face of losses, but it would receive no more Federal help. Should Pennsylvania decide in the first place not to participate in the program, the alcohol tax revenues would simply continue to come to the Federal government.

Why so complex an approach? The revolving fund encourages good management, because bad management drains the fund and automatically disestablishes the program. Providing the money to establish the fund by ceding tax rights from the Federal to state or local levels minimizes the opportunities for Federal bureaucracies to feed off the program. Ceding the tax rights only for the specific purposes of the program keeps the Federal government's purpose in control and in focus, while giving the states an incentive to participate. The reversion of the tax rights after the initial "lump" of money to start the fund going has been provided prevents the program from turning into an endless drain on the Federal budget—an important consideration in the face of the Federal deficit.

We think such revolving funds are a promising way to permit Federal government activism in support of culturally conservative policies while minimizing bureaucracy. We recognize they will have some problems in practice, as everything does, and that others may discover better ways to achieve the desired ends. When they do, we will welcome and adopt them.

The one thing that is fixed in our agenda is the overall goal of recalling Americans to their inherited culture. That culture is still very much alive, in the ways many Americans think and live. It is the long-standing culture of the West, and it is one of mankind's great achievements. It was and can be again a supremely functional culture, in what it creates, builds, and provides. All that has been wanting is our willingness to turn to it.

The remainder of this document offers the beginnings of this turning point in our history as a free people. It is no more than a beginning, an example of the kind of work the task demands. It is also an invitation to others to join the effort. Its further development will require the thoughts and contributions of many people, including many who have not thought of themselves as conservatives. The door to cultural conservatism stands open to thoughtful moderates and liberals, many of whom are coming to see the unfortunate effects of two decades of cultural breakdown. Cultural conservatives welcome the active participation of Democrats as well as Republicans. The concern for the less fortunate that motivates many Democrats is one of Western culture's best traditions.

Every American has something to contribute to build on this beginning. Existing policy areas need new directions; shared goals must be translated into innovative, promising means and experiments; and new areas for policy must be identified and thought through. The well-spring of innovation that has been an American hallmark for two centuries has not run dry. The goal of this paper is to prime the pump.

NOTES

1. Divorce now ends about half of all new American marriages; the birthrate has been below the population replacement (ZPG) level for 17 years; illegitimate births have soared from about 5% of all births in 1960 to over 20% today, and more than a third of these are to teenaged mothers; for every one of these out-of-wedlock teenage pregnancies that end in birth, two end in abortion; for the full statistics, see Michael Novak *et al., The New Consensus on Family and Welfare* (Washington, D.C.: American Enterprise Institute and Marquette University Press, 1987), pp. 135–6, Tables A-13 and A-14.

2. The Center for the Assessment of Educational Progress, in a report titled *The Subtle Danger, Reflections on the Literacy Abilities of America's Young Adults,* January, 1987, found that 44% of our high-school students couldn't use a tax table to find out how much income tax a hypothetical citizen owed; 48% couldn't use an almanac index to find information, and 70% could not write a satisfactory letter complaining of a billing mistake.

3. Burton Yale Pines, *Back to Basics* (New York: Morrow, 1982), chapter 4.

4. To take just one notorious example, when President Kennedy sent to Congress his welfare message in 1962 (a message which would eventually inspire the Great Society programs enacted in his memory), he said that the goal of these programs was to strengthen the family, reduce divorce and illegitimacy, and raise employment.

5. Michael Novak, "The Future of 'Economic Rights'," unpublished paper.

The Family

Many of us have begun to ask again about the role of the family and the critical importance of the values embodied in strong families—discipline, hard work, ambition, and self-sacrifice, patience and love. It's easy enough to mock such values as bourgeois. But middle-class or not, they appear to constitute the spiritual foundation for achievement—the psychological infrastructure, if you will, for both personal growth and full participation in the world around us.

—Clifton R. Wharton[1]

There never was a society throughout all of history . . . without a family as the central unit for launching the education of children, for character formation, and as the moral agent of society.

—Amitai Etzioni[2]

From a culturally conservative perspective, the traditional family—husband, wife and children—is the ultimate expression of the dictum, "form follows function." The family is stronger than all other forms of human organization because it is rooted in the most powerful and universal of human needs: the need to give and receive personal attention, especially in the form of love.

32

Love is the basis of the family. Love unites husband, wife and children into a single unit. It provides the strongest possible underpinning to the self-sacrifice and service to others that a good marriage and the raising of children require. It enables individuals to overcome the friction inherent in all personal relationships, and so provide a stable home, so necessary to the well-being of both parents and children. The nature of man is such that no other institution—no commune, no professional service, no school, no church, nothing—can possibly substitute for the family.

Love is also the family's first function. Without love, few individuals are able to find life rewarding or satisfying. The complex interactions that build among individuals permanently united as husband, wife and children allow love its greatest scope. A society in which the family is weak will be a society in which few individuals can find or give the love they need for fulfillment.

This function alone, so central to the well-being of every person, would justify regarding the family with reverence. But it is not the family's only vital function. Another is the education of children. While formal education is an important part of this process, the influence of a school is far smaller than the influence of a home in a child's development. As Dr. Martin Luther King, Jr., said, "the group consisting of mother, father and child (is) the main educational agency of mankind."[3]

The reason the family is so central to education is that the family, more than any other agency, instills virtues and molds a child's character. The child's ability to achieve, in school as well as in later life, depends heavily on his values and character. A recent report of the Department of Education, *The Family: Preserving America's Future*, notes,

Experts have watched in astonishment as the children of
the (Asian) "boat people" who just a few years ago
arrived penniless and facing language and cultural impediments have catapulted themselves literally to the "top of
the class." On national standardized tests of academic
achievement, 27 percent of the refugee children scored in
the 90th percentile on math achievement. In grade point
average, more than a quarter of them had an "A-average"
and overall their scholastic average was 3.05 or slightly
above a "B." Research shows that the reason for this
performance is the values the children bring with them.
Nathan Caplan of the University of Michigan found these
children possessed traditional cultural values, a cohesive
family structure and achievement orientation.[4]

Clearly, what these children had learned in the home was
the basis of their astonishing achievements in school.

The educational role of the family is of key importance
in two particular respects. The first is helping people
escape from poverty. The child who is reared in a stable
but poor family is much more likely to be able to rise out
of poverty than is a child reared in an impoverished
single-parent home.[5] The stable family is more likely to
assist the child to develop a sound character, functional
values, and marketable work habits and skills. Children
need both male and female role models. The child without a father is at a serious disadvantage. As one study
notes:

Raised in an environment in which fathers don't provide
for their young and dependency on government is assumed, few children will develop the skills of self-sufficiency, or even the concept of personal responsibility.
Young men will not strive to be good providers and young
women will not expect it of their men. Family breakdown
becomes cyclical, out-of-wedlock births become cyclical.
And the culture of poverty grows.[6]

A second key educational role of the family is developing a sense of civic virtue. As the Founders of this nation knew, democracy depends on a strong sense of civic virtue in the citizenry. A nation that casts off the imposed discipline of an authoritarian government depends on its people's self-discipline: their willingness to sacrifice for the common good, to vote for the nation's interest over their own, and to build for the common future. As *The Family* states:

> The framers of our Constitution saw clearly that only those societies strong in certain civic virtues could sustain an experiment in representative democracy. The family is the primary training ground for individual responsibility, for self-sacrifice, for seeking a common goal rather than self-interest. Without those virtues, democracy breaks down in an unrestrained battle of each against the other. Only strong families can build a society strong enough to make representative democracy secure.[7]

The family's third vital function is both broad and deep. Put simply, the family is the basis of a civilized society. The motivations which drive men and women to do what must be done if society is to prosper—to work, to produce, to delay gratification, to save and invest, to create pleasant, safe towns and neighborhoods, to fight crime and corruption, and to defend the nation when it is attacked—are rooted primarily in the family. The family is, in this sense, the bedrock of civilization. It is what leads people—especially men, some argue[8]—to build and protect order, peace and prosperity, and to prefer civilization to barbarism. Self-interest can often be accommodated in an atmosphere of turbulence and unrest, of disorder and violence. But such an atmosphere is a threat to the other members of a family, and the quality a family brings out best—looking to the well-being of others—leads people to prefer order and peace, to prefer civilization.

These three functions—providing a place where love can flourish; educating children, which is to say, providing for the culture's continuation over time; and providing the basis of civilization itself—are of such importance as to earn the family a highly honored place as the basic societal unit. Government and society owe it respect and support—both of which have often been missing in recent years. Again, *The Family* puts it best:

> It is time to reaffirm some "home truths" and to restate the obvious. Intact families are good. Families who choose to have children are making a desirable decision. Mothers and fathers who then decide to spend a good deal of time raising those children themselves rather than leaving it to others are demonstrably doing a good thing for those children. Countless Americans do these things every day. They ask for no special favors—they do these things naturally out of love, loyalty and a commitment to the future. They are the bedrock of our society. Public policy and the culture in general must support and reaffirm these decisions—not undermine and be hostile to them or send a message that we are neutral. . . . Neither prosperity nor freedom can be sustained without a transfusion, from generation to generation, of family values: respect and discipline, restraint and self-sacrifice, interdependence and cooperation, loyalty and fidelity, and an ethical code that gives to individuals, however lowly, a transcendent import.[9]

A few decades ago, most people would have agreed with these arguments in favor of the traditional family—as most do today. But they would also have been puzzled: why is it necessary to make the argument? The

traditional family was so common as to be almost universal. Most people got married and had children; a person
married once, for life; children were born in wedlock,
and grew up in a stable family; the father was the
breadwinner, and the mother stayed home to devote
herself to raising the children. Most of us who are over
40 grew up in such a society and in such a family.

No longer. Today, it is necessary to make the case for
the traditional family because it is disappearing. Many
people no longer marry, or marry but choose to have no
children—a choice frequently made because of economic
pressure. The divorce rate is running about 50% for the
generation now under thirty. Illegitimate birth is common, especially among the inner-city poor; such births
have increased by 450% as a percentage of all births in
the past 30 years.[10] Almost half of non-white babies are
born out of wedlock. Forty-one percent of all mothers
work outside the home full-time; according to some
polls, close to half of the working women with small
children—and almost one-quarter of such women now
work full-time—would prefer to stay home to care for
their children but cannot afford to. One social scientist,
observing the trends, stated, "If we continue to disman-
tle our American family at the accelerating pace we have
been doing so since 1965, there will not be a single
American family left by the year 2008."[11]

What forces have been tearing the traditional family
apart?

• Stagnant or falling living standards. Despite reassur-
ing government statistics that show rising income, more
and more families have found they need two incomes to
maintain a middle-class standard of living—even while
accepting reduced standards of housing, transportation,
and education for their children.

• The loss of social sanctions against permissive sex. Premarital sex lies behind the explosion of illegitimacy and abortion. Extra-marital sex is a prime destroyer of marriages and families.

• Government action. Until recently, the family was a respected legal entity. But in the past two decades, a series of court decisions have attempted to deny the family a legal existence.[12] Parental rights to guide their childrens' upbringing have been undermined by government rulings. Taxes on families have risen tremendously; between 1960 and 1984, the average tax rate for a family with two children climbed 43%.[13] The personal exemption fell to one-eighth of its former value between 1948 and 1984.

• Abortion. The growing demand for abortion expresses a morality in which the highest good is short-term personal convenience. When that morality invades other aspects of family life, such as behavior toward a marriage partner, values inculcated in children, and acceptance of responsibilities toward aging parents, it is highly destructive.

• A definition of the family by some government leaders in a metaphorical rather than a concrete sense. The decline of the traditional family has aroused sufficient concern to lead many politicians to take a "pro-family" position. However, there is sometimes less here than meets the eye. A careful reading shows that, in a number of cases, the "family" being defended is a metaphorical "family of man" or the community as a "family." While such sentiments are noble, they are sometimes misleading, in that those espousing them continue to support policies destructive to actual, concrete families under the cover of their "pro-family" rhetoric. This confuses and diverts the movement to support and restore the traditional family.

• Divorce. In the late 1960s and early 1970s, with little forethought and virtually no debate, the United States radically revised its divorce laws. The passage by virtually every state, beginning with California in 1969, of "no fault" divorce legislation was hailed as a liberating advance that would remove much of the pain and acrimony from divorce. The premise of no-fault divorce laws is that the decision to dissolve a marriage is one without moral content—and that the terms of dissolution should focus exclusively on such practical matters as division of property and custody of children.

After 17 years of experience in California and nearly as much in the other states, few will openly defend the divorce revolution any longer. Opposition that at first was intuitive, and later became anecdotal, has long since become quantifiable, thanks to the work of such scholars as Lenore Weitzman. No-fault divorce has worsened the lot of women, rewarded deserters (usually men, whose average income increases 42 per cent after divorce), and hit hard at the most vulnerable members of families—children and those who take care of them (usually mothers whose average income is reduced by 73%).[14] The divorce rate has not paused in its upward ascent.

Some proposed remedies for this social disaster, such as strict enforcement of child support laws, are purely material in nature and command wide support. But if the remedies are purely economic, a fundamental misunderstanding about the nature of marriage and the family will continue. Cultural conservatives believe that marriage and children have vital social functions, and that divorce is therefore a public evil, however understandable or inevitable in some cases. If divorce is in fact a public evil, the concept of fault must be reintroduced to divorce law in the states. Fault should influence support, property settlements, and custody, at a bare minimum. In addition, and as perhaps the most urgently needed re-form, divorce should stop being routinely available to a single partner. Normally, divorce should be available by mutual consent only, unless fault is proven by the suer. And it should be available only after good-faith attempts at reconciliation have proven futile.

Because lifelong marriage and the traditional family are good, society should return to a policy of making divorce difficult, and the partner who provokes it fully accountable by law.

• Pornography. By portraying women—and children—as mere objects for the gratification of lurid desires, pornographic materials have blinded many people to the nature of the male-female relationship and to the basic dignity of the human person. All too often, direct attacks on the family, such as child molesting and sexual assault, have been found to be linked to obsessive use of obscene materials.[15]

All of these factors have contributed, and continue to contribute, to the dissolution of the traditional family. In view of the family's vital role in society, that dissolution must be stopped, and reversed. That leads us to our goals.

Goals

• Restore the traditional, stable family, where one parent is normally in the home, as the environment in which the vast majority of children are raised.

• Reduce the incidence of divorce, out-of-wedlock pregnancy, abortion, and pre-marital sex.

• Promote broad acceptance of the values on which stable families depend, including responsibilities to and for offspring, disapproval of extra-marital sex, and reverence for life, both before and after birth.

• Restore the legal standing of the family, including presumption of the reasonableness of parental action, and void legislative, administrative and judicial actions which work to undermine the traditional family.

• Restore the economic well-being of the family by making it possible for single wage-earner families to maintain a middle-class standard of living.

• Replace governmental neutrality (or worse) toward the traditional family with government recognition of its vital functional roles.

Means and Experiments

1. Restore the personal exemption to its original (1948) value. Though recently raised to $2,000, its original value would be approximately $5,000 in today's dollars. However, this change should apply only to dependents.

2. Make the current child-care credit universal, so that parents who care for their own children receive the same tax benefits as those who rely on substitute care such as day-care centers.

3. Permit employers to offer a "family wage," that is, a higher wage to heads of families, reflecting their need to provide for others. The 1966 Department of Labor regulation forbidding employers to pay higher salaries to heads of families should be withdrawn, as should any other legal impediments.

4. Encourage states to eliminate "no-fault" divorce.

5. Where children are present in a marriage, they could be assigned their own guardian *ad litem* in any divorce action sought by their parents; it would be the function of this guardian to represent the children's interest in having their parents remain together.

6. In cases where divorce is granted:

    a) Eliminate the presumption that custody of minor children should go to the mother. In view of the psychological evidence that young children deprived of their same-sex parent are at greater risk for deviancy in later life, judges should consider awarding custody of male children to the father and female children to the mother.

    b) Depending on the grounds for the divorce, structure support payments so as to maintain the standard of living of the partner who did not seek divorce.

    c) Define assets such as professional education, job security, and enhanced earning capacity achieved during a marriage as joint property.

    d) Award lump-sum alimony to a partner whose sacrifices have led to increased earning power for the other.

    e) Enforce the collection of support payments, defining non-support as felonious child neglect.

7. In states where "no-fault" laws remain on the books, a marriage "contract" could be offered as an alternative to the normal marriage license. Couples could choose a contract under which they could not end their marriage on a "no-fault" basis.

8. Legalize education in the home, with appropriate safeguards, e.g., periodic standardized tests administered by the local schools.

9. Pass a constitutional amendment giving legal standing to the family. The purpose of the amendment would be to restore the common law recognition of the family as a legal entity accepted until recently by the courts.

10. Expand the current, broad-based "Say no" cam-

paign, now focused on drug use, to include pre-marital sex.

11. Prohibit state, including public school, involvement in explicit and value-free sex education—and in any sex education without parental consent.

12. Overturn or reverse *Roe v. Wade* in such a way that appropriate legislation can at least prohibit abortion on demand. While it is undoubtedly true that outlawing abortion on demand will not stop all abortions, it will make them far less common. Of equal importance, prohibiting this act will make it clear that society, and government as its agent, does not approve of a morality which sacrifices one person's life to the short-term convenience of another.

13. To encourage mothers to bring their children into the world, the system for adoption should be strengthened and expanded. Pregnant women who do not wish to keep their baby should have easy access to an adoption center, with assurance that a home will be found for the child, and that confidentiality will be preserved.

14. Enforce Federal and state laws against obscenity and child pornography. While further legislative improvements can be helpful, the real need is for enforcement of laws already on the books. The Supreme Court has consistently ruled that obscenity enjoys no protection under the First Amendment.

NOTES

1. Clifton R. Wharton, Rockefeller Foundation Chairman, Chancellor of the State University of New York, "Demanding Families and Black Achievement," *Education Week,* October 29, 1986, quoted in *The Family:* Preserving America's Future, a report of the Working Group on the Family, November, 1986

(report available from the U.S. Department of Education), p. 21.

2. Amitai Etzioni, testimony before the U.S. Senate Subcommittee on Family and Human Services, "Broken Families: Overview and Effect on Children," March 22, 1983, quoted in *Ibid.*, p. 10.

3. *Ibid.*, p. 23.

4. *Ibid.*, p. 58.

5. See Michael Novak et al., *The New Consensus on Family and Welfare* (Washington, D.C.: American Enterprise Institute, 1987), pp. 17 and 25.

6. Charles Murray, "According to Age—Longitudinal Profiles of AFDC Recipients and the Poor by Age Group," Institute for Public Policy Studies, University of Michigan, September, 1986; quoted in *Ibid.*, p. 32.

7. *Ibid.*, p. 13.

8. See George Gilder, *Men and Marriage*, Pelican Publishing, Gretna, LA, 1986.

9. *The Family*, p. 5.

10. *Ibid.*, p. 8.

11. Amitai Etzioni, *op. cit.*, quoted in *Ibid.*, p. 18.

12. *Ibid.*, pp. 14–17.

13. *Ibid.*, p. 60.

14. Cited by Marianne Takas, "Divorce: Who Gets the Blame in 'No Fault'?" *Ms*, February 1986, p. 48–50; quoted in *Ibid.*, p. 19.

15. A wide range of police reports are surveyed in *Final Report of the Attorney General's Commission on Pornography* (Washington: U.S. Department of Justice, 1986).

Education

I venture to submit to you . . .

that during the past 40 to 50 years those who are
responsible for education have progressively removed
from the curriculum of studies the Western culture which
produced the modern democratic state;

that the schools and colleges have, therefore, been
sending out into the world men who no longer understand
the creative principle of the society in which they must
live;

that, deprived of their cultural tradition, the newly
educated Western men no longer possess in the form and
substance of their own minds and spirits, the ideas, the
premises, the rationale, the logic, the method, the values,
or the deposited wisdom which are the genius of the
development of Western civilization;

that the prevailing education is destined, if it continues,
to destroy Western civilization and is in fact destroying
it;

that our civilization cannot effectively be maintained
where it still flourishes or be restored where it has been
crushed without the revival of the central, continuous,
and perennial culture of the Western world; and that,
therefore, what is now required in the modern educational
system is not the expansion of its facilities or the specific
reform of its curriculum and administration but a thorough reconsideration of its underlying assumptions and
of its purposes.

—Walter Lippmann[1]

A cultural conservative's approach to education begins with that quotation from Lippmann's Phi Beta Kappa address of 1940. Education must be concerned with our "perennial culture," because we cannot afford to lose it.

There is a two-way relationship between the working values of our society and the culture which contains our "classics." In one direction, the classics enrich and inform the popular culture. Compared to our everyday perceptions, the classics of Western literature hold out a broader and deeper understanding of the human condition. The classics of architecture, music, and painting hold out richer prospects for enjoyment and more enduring standards of beauty. The monuments of our country—both tangible ones, like the Liberty Bell and the text of the Constitution, and figurative ones, like our collective images of the immigrant and the pioneer—summon us to remember where we have been historically and who we are resolved to be among the nations.

At the same time, in the opposite direction, it is the values, habits, and thoughts of ordinary people which sustain these classics in broad esteem, allowing us to hold onto them as things still meaningful, and dip into them as things still intelligible.

Without this two-way relationship, a people has no heritage. When the classics that once formed it are cast off as obsolete finery, the elites drift with fashion, and the people are led by sloganeers.

Education, if it is to be worthy of the name, must enable this two-way relationship to continue and to bear fruit. It may be civilization's single most important task, for the simple reason that at root, education *is* civilization. Education is a civilization perpetuating itself.

Appropriately, the most important part of education is entrusted to societys most vital institution: the family.

Basic attitudes, character, oppenness to and interest in ideas, the ground rules by which a person thinks and lives—are all formed in the family. Schools play an important role in building on the base which the family provides, but no school can provide the base by itself. If the family fails to perform its educational functions, the school's task is almost hopeless.[2] In a very real sense, therefore, education policy must begin with family policy—a fact reflected in the preceding section.

Beyond the family, education depends heavily on schooling. Because the classics of our culture come to us "encoded" in words, notes, symbols, and artistic conventions, which need to be learned, and because neither learning nor any other serious endeavor is possible without good traits of character, the schools have three central functions. Two help build the base for education: providing basic skills and building character. The third is education itself.

Primary and secondary schools bear the burden of providing basic skills: reading, writing, mathematics, ability to reason, verbal communication in standard English, and, today, basic computer skills. Unfortunately, our public schools do not do this job nearly as well as they did several decades ago. The average high school graduate is less well prepared in basic skills than were his parents and grandparents.[3] The decline has been measurable since 1964, when standardized test scores began to fall; since 1970, average SAT scores have dropped 8% in English and almost 5% in mathematics.[4] Less measurable but more critical is the fact that many high school graduates are functional illiterates.[5] Society must recognize that a decline in basic skill levels will translate into declines in almost everything else.

The task of character building rests primarily on the family, but schools also have an important role to play.

They must reinforce and inculcate specific virtues such as punctuality, impulse control, respect for legitimate authority, and sound work habits. Educational "experimentalists" have sometimes said that rules and norms would "inhibit" the children, but classroom practices which neglected these virtues have repeatedly failed. As a result, the function of these character traits has become more and more obvious: without them, students do not learn the basic academic skills.[6]

But basic morals are equally functional: respect for life, honesty, courage, a sense of right and wrong, kindness, compassion, etc. They create the sort of society which will endure, and they prepare students for life beyond the school. Secretary of Education William Bennett put it well:

> If we want our children to possess the traits of character we most admire, we need to teach them what those traits are. They must learn to identify the forms and contents of those traits. They must achieve at least a minimal level of moral literacy that will enable them to make sense of what they will see in life and, we may hope, that will help them to live it well.

One might add that, to the extent we fail to teach such values as honesty and compassion, we lay the basis for a society neither honest nor compassionate.

In basic values as in skills, the quality of teaching has declined over the past several decades. As recently as the early 1960s, most schools taught values. Report cards often listed such subjects as citizenship, responsibility, work habits, and punctuality. Reading lessons, discussions about our nation's history, and other classroom exercises often told a tale about morals. The Ten Commandments were often posted in the classroom. Few children of earlier generations forgot George Washington's "I cannot tell a lie."

In the 1960s and 1970s, this largely disappeared. Radical educational theories (prime examples of cultural radicalism) played a key role in the disappearance. It was said that minority-group children would be "damaged" by exposure to majority values. Teachers were warned that all values were equally personal, hence none should be "imposed" or taught.[7] Some used a "values clarification" approach, in which ethics was replaced by substanceless "values" such as "openness," "pluralism," and respect for "diversity," which seemed easier to teach because they avoided the line between right and wrong.

But the most destructive influence of all was the dissolution of discipline in many public schools. Without discipline, any attempt to teach traditional values quickly became a mockery, because the school could not practice what it preached. Those who flouted the values the school taught got away with it, and laughed at those too timid to follow them. Anyone who stuck with the old ways looked like a dupe, a nerd, "uncool." Indeed, without discipline, it quickly became evident that nothing could be taught—neither values nor skills. The schools simply fell apart.

In the last few years, a spreading "back to basics" movement in the public schools has begun to bring improvements both in discipline and in the teaching of skills. SAT scores bottomed out in 1982, and have been rising gradually since. Parents' concerns, especially about drugs in the schools, have brought stronger discipline in many school districts. Parents have become more involved in their schools' policies and also in supporting school discipline with renewed discipline in the home.

Many students have welcomed the reforms, because they want to have a chance to learn.[8]

But the teaching of morals remains weak. For the most part, public schools still teach in a vacuum of values, and character development as part of public education is ignored. The focus is entirely on skill-related "content," and the notion that cultural and moral literacy are as important as technical literacy is considered outdated, unprofessional, or too controversial.[9]

Providing basic skills and developing character lay the basis for education, but they do not build the edifice. What is education?

True education is what is sometimes called a classical education. It is far more than training. It is devoted to developing an understanding of reality, in all its dimensions, through the best insights that civilization has to offer. It means becoming familiar with the West's great literature, ideas, thinkers and authors, from the classical Greeks and Biblical prophets forward to our own time. It involves the study of history, literature, religion, and philosophy, the substance of our culture, and also logic, the tool for thinking. It includes science and mathematics, not just to make scientists, but to teach the disciplined mode of inquiry science requires. Its goal is a civilized person: someone who poses the great questions, understands the great answers, and knows why they are great—someone who sees the world whole and grasps his own place in it.

While secondary schools certainly should contribute to education defined this way, the full job belongs to colleges and universities. Unfortunately, too many colleges allow their students to graduate without being exposed even to a core curriculum which includes the classics. They have become mere skill factories, teaching students the things they need to get a job—vocational schools for the middle classes.

The role of education should first be to do what its name implies: to "lead the student out" of his or her small, private world, into the larger world of a great civilization. This role is unfulfilled when great ideas are allowed to be forgotten, the great authors left unread. When our colleges and universities concentrate only on teaching marketing or pre-law, they do their students— and ultimately the nation—a great disservice.[10]

Goals

• Recognize that family policy is inherently a part of education policy. A strong family, focused on its traditional task of raising children, is a *sine qua non* of effective education of the next generation.

• Restore public education to the point where skill levels of high school graduates are at least as high as they were in the past.

• Re-establish strong discipline in all schools, especially those serving economically disadvantaged communities, where crime has been a problem and where discipline is needed as a basis for climbing out of poverty.

• Reincorporate the teaching of traditional morals and character development into public education, recognizing that cultural and moral literacy are equal in importance with technical literacy.

• Reform undergraduate education to include at least some exposure to the essential elements of a classical education.

Means and Experiments

1. To help insure that local school authorities are accountable and that the voters are informed, districts

should be encouraged to administer standardized achievement tests shortly before school board elections are held. Parents would thereby be enabled to compare their schools' current performance with both their own past performance and other school districts as a guide in voting.

2. Strong efforts should be made to restore the legal right of principals and teachers to impose punishment (including reasonable corporal punishment) on defiant students, and to search both them and their possessions when necessary, without fear of legal liability. All public school systems should provide for the expeditious expulsion of habitual disrupters and other serious offenders.

3. The level of discipline should figure prominently in assessments by certification boards that periodically visit public schools. Repeated criminal acts in a school should lead to its decertification.

4. State government leaders should mandate higher standards for state college and university admission. This would complement recent actions in some states to raise qualifications for high school graduation.

5. Since competition will not only be healthy for the public schools but will also help to break the monopoly influence of educational ideologues, Congress and the state legislatures should move expeditiously to approve broad-based voucher plans.

6. The Graduate Record Examination should be reformed to reflect stiffer requirements in the mastery of classical authors, the major Western philosophers, and other topics central to the assimilation of our culture.

7. Colleges and universities that receive Federal financial assistance should be required to include a core curriculum reflecting a classical education in their undergraduate program. The private accrediting agencies, not the government, should determine whether an institution

has met the requirement, so as to preclude any government role in setting curricula.

8. The President should provide leadership in soliciting private funding to establish scholarships to support post-graduate training in specialized fields for graduates of full four-year classical education programs (such as the "Great Books" programs). The object should be to eliminate any financial burden on those who devote their undergraduate years to receiving an education, and thereby postpone special-field training.

9. At the same time, current student loan aid programs should be reformed. Students receiving Federal financial assistance should be required to meet high academic standards in terms of course load and grade point average. Federal student aid should come as part of a work-study program which requires in effect a "matching contribution" from the student. The object in both cases is not to reduce aid levels but to insure a serious commitment on the part of the student receiving assistance.

10. Civil service examinations for candidates for top-level civil service positions should be re-structured to test for the qualities and abilities of a classically educated man or woman.

11. To insure that teachers know the subject matter they are to teach, they should be subject to periodic competency testing.

12. Other states should be encouraged to adopt the teacher recruitment approach of New Jersey, where anyone holding an A.B. degree from an accredited college or university may teach in public schools. They need only pass a competency test and receive a two-week orientation to classroom teaching. By breaking the monopoly which education departments hold over teacher certification, New Jersey's approach gives talented peo-

ple from all walks of life the same chance to serve and innovate in public education as they have long enjoyed in private education.

NOTES

1. "Education vs. Western Civilization," *The American Scholar,* Spring, 1941.

2. See Home and School Institute, Inc., *The Forgotten Factor in School Success—The Family,* 1985.

3. "In one telling experiment designed to compare today's high school education with that of previous generations, freshmen entering the University of Minnesota in 1978 were given a reading exam that had been taken by freshmen a half-century earlier. The result: the 1978 grades were decidedly lower than the 1928's; in fact even the best contemporary students did not perform as well as the best of 1928," Burton Yale Pines, *Back to Basics* (New York: Morrow, 1982), p. 101.

4. See Willard Wirtz et al., *Report of the Advisory Panel on the Scholastic Aptitude Test Score Decline,* College Entrance Examination Board, New York, 1977. Many analysts believe that these numbers understate the real decline, because the test itself has been gradually made easier.

5. Persons are considered functionally illiterate when they read with such difficulty (and reluctance) that they cannot cope with newspapers, maps, and other printed items in everyday use. In 1979, 13% of our 17 year olds *who were still in high school* were found to be in this category. Among dropouts the percentage would presumably have been higher. See Pines, *loc. cit.*

In fact, however, the idea of 'functional illiteracy' has been so narrowly defined that it doesn't begin to capture the extent of the incompetence among our young people. The Center for the Assessment of Educational Progress recently tested teenagers for their ability to perform tasks that required not only reading but using the information in a series of connected steps. The results were catastrophic. 32% couldn't record a simple phone message. 56% couldn't make a simple division to find out how much a given jar of peanut butter cost per ounce. 70% couldn't write a letter of complaint to a company that had misbilled them. CAEP, *The Subtle Danger, Reflections on the Literacy Ability of America's Young Adults* (Report No. 16-CAEP-01; January, 1987). Private industry has found the same thing. According to the Washington *Post*, August 24, 1987, the New York Telephone Company tested about 23,000 applicants this year for entry-level jobs, such as telephone operators. 84% failed.

6. See Amitai Etzioni, *An Immodest Agenda* (New York: McGraw-Hill, 1983), chapter 6, "Schools: Educational Experiences First"; Edward A. Wynne and Herbert J. Walberg, "The Complementary Goals of Character Development and Academic Excellence," *Educational Leadership,* December 1985/January 1986.

7. It is helpful to observe that the term 'values' is ambiguous in current usage. Sometimes it means morals, and sometimes it means choices (that is, the goals or goods someone has chosen to pursue with special dedication, as in a profession, career, or plan of life). These meanings are not the same, since people can dedicate themselves to different goods and careers while sharing the same morals. The fact that the word 'values' covers both meanings has lead many cultural radicals to imagine that morals are somehow a matter of choice, as though we had to choose a morality before it was "in force" for us. People do not seem to notice that, if this idea were true, the Nazis did nothing wrong.

8. See, for example, James C. Enochs, *The Restoration of Standards: The Modesto Plan* (Wayne State University Chapter of Phi Beta Kappa, 1979); U.S. Department of Education, *What Works,* 1986.

9. The lack of emphasis on cultural literacy is now yielding results which literally defy belief. In a recent NEH survey of 8,000 high school juniors, it was revealed that 68% could not place the Civil War within the correct half century. A third thought that Columbus discovered the New World after 1750.

Two thirds failed to recognize even one salient fact about Dostoyevski, Faulkner, Melville, Dante, Hawthorne, Whitman, or Chaucer. See Lynne V. Cheney, *American Memory: A Report on the Humanities in the Nation's Public Schools,* forthcoming. The results were reported in the Washington *Post*, August 31, 1987, p. A1.

10. This point has been made with unprecedented power by Allan Bloom in his recent best-seller, *The Closing of the American Mind,* subtitled, *How Higher Education Has Failed Democracy and Impoverished the Souls of Today's Students* (New York: Simon and Shuster, 1987).

Institutional Design

We should not be allowed to discover "political failures" because we have succeeded in isolating the self-seeking behavior of politicians and bureaucrats and, at the same time, be unconcerned about the "market failures" that show up because of externalities.

—James M. Buchanan[1]

Institutional design is a new issue defined by cultural conservatism. It pertains to the culture that develops in each office, company, or government department. There is a mutually reinforcing relationship (some would call it a feedback loop) between the way the institution is designed and the kind of culture that is fostered in it. Why must this become a national issue? Because poor institutional design is a major reason why so many of our institutions seem not to work, and why we no longer compete effectively in many fields.

What is institutional design? It is the structure of jobs and the pattern of relations between job holders inside an institution: a corporation, government department, university, military unit, etc. Cultural conservatives contend that the kind of behavior the design rewards must agree with certain traditional values if the institution is to be productive—and that this holds true whether the institution is in the private sector or in the public sector.[2]

In conventional economic and political thought, little attention has been paid to institutional design. It was not assumed to have a role in affecting values and motivations. These were thought to be a product of the sector in which the institution was located. In a private, for-profit company, job-holders were assumed to be motivated by commercial success. The competitive goal and nature of the institution was thought to be mirrored in the decision-making of those inside it: they would be aggressive in advancing the company's product because it coincided with their own self-interest. By contrast, in the public sector, job-holders were assumed to be motivated by the public interest. The legislative mandate and public nature of the department or agency was thought to be mirrored in the decision-making of those working in it: they would be public-spirited in advancing the social purpose of the institution.

These assumptions have colored people's thinking on both sides of the political spectrum. People on the left have noticed the self-interested agents in the marketplace failing to address certain social problems because they saw no profit in doing so, and have created government programs to meet those problems, serene in the confidence that the agents working in the programs would be public-spirited. Government would not only fill the gaps left by "market failure" but would fill them well. People on the right, led by the same assumptions but by different perceptions of what was a "problem," feared bureaucrats as dangerous ideological purists or else as drones who were so public-spirited that they didn't understand how the world works and couldn't get anything done. The solution would be to fire them all or, failing that, to replace them with executives from the private sector, who understood efficiency.

Both sides have tended to be disappointed. Government agencies seem to grow according to internal incentives of their own, while the social problems remain. Inefficiencies long attributed to government workers seem to be spreading in the corporate world as well. The importation of private executives into government service looks like a slow game of musical chairs, in which listless managers circulate from sector to sector, disinclined to innovate in either.

An important part of the reason for these disappointing results has been brought to light by public choice theory.[3] Our conventional assumptions about how people are motivated and how they will behave has been exposed as fallacious. There is a fundamental distinction between predicting how people will act (a descriptive task) and judging how they *ought* to act (a prescriptive task). We have tended to mix these two together. Economic rationality ought, perhaps, to determine what companies and their workers do, but will it? Established public policies ought to determine what government workers do, but will they? From a different angle, it is often conceded that moral norms and public goals belong to the prescriptive sphere of what ought to be done, whereas the real world (what will be done) is dominated by self-interest. But if this is true, government agents are no more public-spirited than the rest of us, and there will be "government failures" and "externalities" to match all the market's failures. Public choice theory demands that we learn to be consistent in our assumptions.

Cultural conservatives meet this challenge by recognizing that how people *will* behave in their jobs depends upon the real motivations and incentives built into the design of the institution in which they work, no matter in which sector it is located. Hence we pay attention to the basic models for such design.

There are in fact two basic institutional models: the

bureaucratic and the corporative. Most of today's institutions, public and private, follow the bureaucratic model. In a bureaucracy, the institution's overall goals and purposes—what it is supposed to do in the outside, competitive world—are broken down into smaller and smaller pieces until each is small enough to be one person's job. This job may be fitting a taillight on a car on a production line, or managing a department in a store, or commanding an infantry battalion, or commenting on a town's request for a federal grant.

All the jobs in an organization are supposedly linked together in a great chain that ends up producing an outcome or product. But each person is kept rigidly within his job. If he reaches out beyond it—if, say, the worker on the assembly line suggests that the taillight he is putting on the car is not very well designed—he is quickly slapped down. Often, he is penalized for having "rocked the boat," despite widespread recognition that his point was valid. The organization is designed primarily to keep everyone "in their place," i.e. working only within the confines of their particular job.

Faced with this stultifying attitude, what does the person who works in a bureaucracy do? He cannot think about what his company or government department is supposed to accomplish in the outside world—he is told that is not his job. But he still needs goals, purposes, and values. Because he cannot share those of his organization as a whole, he tends to develop his own. One is usually personal career success: moving up the corporate ladder. Another, which is powerful even though subtle, is a tendency to see as most important those things which take most of his time.

Where does the time go in a large company or a government department? Not into work directly concerned with the company's or department's purpose in the outside world, but into problems *inside* the firm or department. Most of the time of people inside bureaucracies goes into dealing with the office immediately above or below them, with the neighboring division, with the competing program or assembly line or department. These internal matters, because they consume so much time, gradually take on controlling importance in the minds of those inside the organization. Once this happens on a general basis—once intra-institutional matters come to dominate an organization's decisions—the organization ceases to be effective.

Conservatives have long recognized what bureaucratic behavior does in government. But the same thing happens in the private sector. As more and more companies have become bureaucracies, we have lost the ability to compete.[4]

The problem has been made worse by the fact that both industries and government departments must now operate in a rapidly changing world. Bureaucracies adjust poorly to change because their internal design prevents them from being focused on the outside world in which the change is occurring. Change upsets all the carefully constructed arrangements inside the organization. It becomes difficult to "slice up the pie" of the budget and of high-prestige responsibilities in the customary way. As they say in the military, it "upsets all the rice bowls." So change is slow and difficult, and outside events move faster than change inside the institution.

Inability to focus on the outside world and poor adaptability to change are only two of the costs of bureaucracy. Another is the psychological price paid by people who are trapped inside a bureaucracy. Today, more and more of us find ourselves in this situation. We go to work wanting to do a good job, wanting to suggest improvements, but the company or the union or the government department will not let us. "Shut up about it. Don't rock the boat. That's the way 'they' want it," we are told. Most of us do not like this advice. We want to use our intelligence and initiative to help the company or department be more competitive. But we are told we cannot do that, or we will ruin our chances for promotion. So we come to hate our job. Whether we are auto workers or businessmen or military officers, we feel we are caught up in a system that has something horribly wrong with it. But we can see no way out. So we go through the motions, playing the game to the degree we must to keep our jobs, and try not to care.

Yet strange as it may seem, some people thrive in this environment. The best term for them is "courtiers."[5] A courtier knows just how to flatter the boss, project the right image, and manipulate other people for his own gain. He knows how to dress for success, he uses just the right tone of voice, and he is always "on the inside." He is usually incompetent at his work, but that is unimportant. In terms of his career, he is highly successful.

The rise of the courtier as an American "type" shows that bureaucracy is not just an efficiency issue. It is also a question of culture. If we look at the kinds of actions a bureaucracy rewards, we see that many are things traditional Western values condemn. First, the "good" bureaucrat is rewarded for being a hypocrite. He is encouraged to pretend to work at creating the product or service his company or government department is supposed to provide, while he really works to keep his own sub-group and his superiors comfortable. Second, he is rewarded for using the people around him—and sacrificing them, if necessary, for his personal advantage. The bureaucrat is encouraged to use people as things, stroking them to his advantage, then throwing them away when they are of no more use to him. Third, the bureaucrat is rewarded for protecting himself by any means available, including betraying those who depend on him. The bureaucrat is given only one commandment: Promote yourself.

Fortunately, there is an alternative to bureaucracy. The alternative is what is called a "corporative" institution. In a corporative institution, people have jobs, but the job means something very different. The institution is designed to get the people inside it to adopt its goals and purposes in the outside world as their *personal* goals and values. It sets values, not just production quotas, and it tries to convince all its employees to adopt these values. It expects all its people to do everything they can, not only in their jobs but beyond their jobs, to advance their common goals and purposes.

Some highly successful businesses, such as Federal Express, are corporative institutions. Management and labor do not see each other as opponents, but as partners working for the same goals. Employees not only do their jobs but also look for ways to do them better. Every person in the company is expected to search for ways to make a better product. When a worker suggests an innovation, management listens to him, appreciates his suggestion and rewards him well.

Why do corporative institutions compete better? If the people inside the institution share the same goals and values—goals and values that support the institution's purpose in the marketplace—there is a check on bureaucratic behavior. When someone starts to cut a deal that will help him or his sub-group but hurt the company's or department's ability to compete, people throughout the organization object. And the senior leadership recognizes their right to object. They are doing what the leadership wants them to: working for the organization's goals and values. Bureaucratic games are cut short.

No approach to setting up an organization will eliminate all self-centered behavior. Human nature does not change. But the corporative approach seems to foster traditional values much better than a bureaucracy does. A corporative organization rewards sincerity, teamwork, and real competence in producing a better product instead of hypocrisy and narrow self-interest. It rewards the real worker, instead of the courtier. Because it rewards such values, it competes more effectively in the outside world.

Goal

• Replace the bureaucratic with the corporative institutional model. We must do this in both the public and the private spheres. We must do it if we want to produce competitive products, help people find satisfying work, and reward ethically and culturally desirable behavior.

Means and Experiments

1. This is a situation where government can do more by exhortation and by example than through legislation. Simply making institutional design an important issue, a subject of thought and discussion throughout the country, would be a major step forward. Government can easily help in this. A Presidential speech on the subject would certainly get attention. Inclusion in Congressional debates and party platforms would help. Individual Members of Congress and other government leaders, including Cabinet members, could "raise consciousness" of the issue substantially by taking it to constituents and other audiences.

2. Perhaps the most powerful tool for government would be force of example. The Federal government should take the lead by transforming its departments into

corporative organizations. This would mean major civil service reform, military reform (the adoption of the corporative model by our armed services is already a major plank in the platform of the military reform movement), and other significant changes in government structure and regulations.

The enhanced performance and better working environment in government departments resulting from the corporative model would affect virtually every American. No longer would dealing with government mean unresponsive civil servants hiding behind reams of forms and regulations, but prompt, pleasant, efficient service. No longer would civil servants and other government employees be told, "Just follow the regulations, don't worry about the result; that's not your job, and you have no authority over it anyway." They would be allowed and encouraged to get good results, results measured in service to the customers—the American public. Almost all Americans now find themselves dealing with the Federal government; few would not notice the change corporative behavior would bring. The argument for adoption of the corporative model by private organizations would be given tremendous impetus by their experience.

3. Government could require from a company's labor representatives and its management a pledge to change from the bureaucratic to the corporative model as a qualification for tariff protection. This is not to say that we generally advocate such protection (see economics section), but only that, if it is granted, a requirement of this kind would increase the chances of its doing some good.

4. Small business loans and other subsidies could be made subject to the same qualification. The difficulty, and it is a formidable one, would be to devise a test of

compliance; but labor unions and private management consultants might be helpful in this.

NOTES

1. "Toward an Analysis of Closed Behavioral Systems," in James M. Buchanan and Robert D. Tollison, eds., *Theory of Public Choice* (Ann Arbor: University of Michigan Press, 1972), p. 23.

2. This chapter is drawn in part from "Bureaucracy: An Inherent Evil?" by Paul M. Weyrich in *Future 21: Directions for America in the 21st Century*, edd. Paul M. Weyrich and Connaught Marshner (Greenwich, Conn.: Devin-Adair, 1984).

3. Buchanan, *op. cit.*, pp. 11–46.

4. See Robert H. Hayes and William J. Abernathy, "Managing Our Way to Economic Decline," *Harvard Business Review* 58 (1980).

5. See Donald Chipman, "The Military Courtier and the Illusion of Competence," *Air University Review*, March–April 1981, pp. 53–62.

Economics

Ill fares the land, to hastening ills a prey,
Where wealth accumulates, and men decay.

—Oliver Goldsmith

Most current conservative thought on economics focuses on growth and on tax, fiscal, monetary and other policies intended to promote faster growth. Cultural conservatives agree that economic growth is highly important and must be a major consideration in economic policy. In our view, economic growth is necessary for fundamental cultural reasons. There is a great cultural difference between a society where the economy is growing and one where it is stagnant or shrinking. In the former, rising living standards, increasing job opportunities, and the availability of capital to entrepreneurs all help create a general sense of optimism. The future looks bright; the society can focus outward, on what it hopes to accomplish; and divergent interests can be accommodated harmoniously as each looks forward to a larger slice of an expanding pie.

In contrast, a society where the economy is stagnant or shrinking tends to turn inward on itself, in a bitter conflict driven by each interest's battle to keep what it has. Pessimism becomes general; the bleakness of the future can lead to extremist political movements; and the overall sense of decline and failure makes it difficult to take new initiatives.[1]

Economic growth plays a special role in American culture. Prosperity is one of the important "glues" that holds our diverse society together. One of the things all Americans have traditionally had in common, regardless of their ethnic group, class origin, or religion, is a belief that life would get better. It would be better for them than it was for their parents, and better for their children than it was for them. Prosperity—steadily increasing prosperity—has always been an important component of this "better."

Because of its diversity, if American society loses this binding agent—the "glue" of shared rising expectations—it risks fragmentation. More homogeneous societies can fall back on race, religion, or other characteristics shared by all their members. Our tradition of individual freedom and limited government provides one such fall-back, but it would clearly be stressed severely if it became our only fully common theme. Seen from this standpoint, prosperity and the economic growth from which it springs take on added importance—a cultural importance that is particularly American.[2]

If cultural conservatives are such strong believers in economic growth, how does their view of economics differ from the usual conservative position? Despite cultural conservatism's strong support for growth, it is not the basis of our economics.[3] To cultural conservatives, the single most important economic principle is the dignity of labor.

While many cultures have regarded work as at best a necessary evil, to be avoided whenever possible by elites, traditional Western culture sees work as a central element in personal fulfillment.[4] It is not simply a regrettable necessity for those without sufficient wealth to live as *rentiers*. On the contrary, few individuals are able to fashion meaningful, rewarding lives for themselves without working. Whether we look at the chronically unemployable or the idle rich, we usually see wasted lives. Therefore, cultural conservative economics begins with work, and the nature and meaning of work is, to us, the most important economic issue.[5]

This view leads not only to a belief in full employment but also to a concern with the quality of the employment—the kinds of jobs available; relations between owners, managers, and workers; working conditions, especially as they foster or deny creativity; the relationship between employment and community; and the opportunities offered a person not just to find any job, but to follow his particular vocation. Cultural conservatives reject all economic concepts that subjugate work and workers and that take a purely instrumental view of labor. Western culture's traditional revulsion toward such concepts was a justifiable reason for much of the opposition to early, exploitative capitalism—to enclosure, sweatshops, piecework, child labor, seven-day weeks, etc.—despite its breakthroughs in the creation of wealth.

We reject all theories which dehumanize labor, such as the capital theory of economic value, "survival of the fittest" social Darwinism (the term was invented not by Darwin but by the social philosopher Herbert Spencer), and Taylorism (the reduction of workers to robot-like repetitive motions on assembly lines). These theories and the practices which have flowed from them undermine support for a free economic order, not because people are opposed to economic freedom, but because they lead to a denigration of work and workers that goes directly against the Western belief in the dignity of all human beings.

The dignity of labor and the need for economic growth are not opposed. Overall economic growth depends, in the long run, on human growth in skills and fulfillment through work. In turn, society's ability to offer high-quality jobs, jobs that offer opportunity for creativity and personal growth, depends on steady economic growth.

The relationship between the dignity of labor and economic growth is in fact symbiotic. History shows this symbiosis clearly. Societies which have achieved growth without at the same time elevating work and workers have failed to sustain the growth. The first mass-based commercial civilization arose not in the West but in medieval China, during the Sung dynasty (960–1270 A.D.) But because Confucian teachings denigrated work, successful merchants often worked only to become non-working landowners and enroll their sons in the government bureaucracy. China's propensity to economic innovation might well have been sustained if its culture had developed respect for work as a means of human fulfillment, rather than exclusively as a means to move on to a non-working status.

This view of work as the basis of economics leads to four other economic principles: fraternity, independence, property rights, and the social function of property.

Fraternity means a sense of a union of goals in society, a realization that the work of each individual is important to and for all. This means that each person, each worker, is concerned about the well-being of all workers, and that every citizen prefers cooperation rather than conflict as a means of attaining society's overall goals.[6] Economic theories which exalt conflict rather than cooperation as the heart of economic activity are inimical to Western culture. Such theories abound both on the left (class conflict) and on the right (social Darwinism). Cultural conservatives reject them, and rejoice that there is an increasing tendency to question their helpfulness to economic efficiency. In our view, social peace and a broad realization that the well-being of each worker is important to the well-being of all is an important aspect of the dignity of labor.

Independence means that an individual is able to support himself and his family through work. Such independence enhances human dignity and the sense of self-worth. Creating economic conditions that offer personally rewarding work to as many people as possible is a major concern of cultural conservatives.

The third principle is popular property rights. Every society has property rights of some kind. But only in Western culture, and not always there, have property rights been made secure for the many. Without the ability to keep the fruits of their labor, those who work have little chance to achieve fulfillment and little incentive to try; instead, stagnation, individual and national, sets in.

In recent years, the lust for expropriation has begun to ebb in the West. Confiscatory tax rates, a *de facto* deprivation of personal property rights, have begun to come down. The United States is a pathbreaker in this regard, having slashed its top income tax rate from 91% in 1963 to 28% in 1988. Other Western countries are moving more slowly, but show signs of following. Reduced tax rates make possible wider distribution of property by encouraging creation of small businesses which in turn create new jobs.

The fourth principle flowing from the dignity of labor is the social function of property. Popular property rights do not mean approval of an individualistic search for self-gratification through greed. They imply a commitment to community, charity, and capital formation. Property rights and giving to those in need have proved compatible here, in the country that has achieved the highest levels of both, the United States. But this relationship is not automatic. Nurturing it is a central goal of cultural conservatism. Darwinian theories of economic life have done grave damage, and the fragile revival of cooperative theories of economic success must continue to go hand in hand with the revival of belief in work and workers as the centers of economic life.

Finally, it must be recognized that every worker is also a consumer. Recent years have seen a revival of interest in the consumer and his rights. Fundamental among them is a right to a currency with long-term stability, so the consumer can choose between immediate consumption and saving. Unfortunately, Western governments continue to deny this right by manipulating their currencies in the name of "demand management," which is to say, they manipulate consumers. At the same time, there has been progress in other areas. Price deregulation of some industries and increased health and safety regulation of others have brought gains to consumers. So has the continuing, if shaky, upholding of free trade. And businesses are gradually moving away from the concept of "planned obsolescence," which forces consumers into unwanted purchases.

The view that work is the most important economic consideration has broad implications. It implies some changes in the way conservatives approach economics, in the attitudes that management and labor have toward each other, in government attitudes toward economic dislocation and change, and in our industries' views of the well-being of other industries. It has negative implications for the bureaucratic model most American companies have adopted. Only by recognizing that work and workers are the beginning of economics can we hope to generate the long-term economic revival the nation clearly requires.

Goals

• Maintain a high long-term rate of economic growth through appropriate macroeconomic and fiscal policies.

• Restructure our practices to reflect the primacy of the dignity of labor. Government, corporate leadership and unions must work together to improve the quality of jobs, with the goal of offering as many people as possible a job that gives room for personal growth, creativity, and fulfillment, including participation in the corporate decision process.

• Government should act to protect personal property rights, especially through avoidance of confiscatory taxation. At the same time, through advocacy, example, and tax incentives, it should promote the principle of the social function of property.

• Define sound currency as a fundamental consumer right.

• Recognize the relationship between employment opportunities and community preservation, with both being clear government goals. This implies an interest in the preservation of traditional industries on which communities depend or their replacement by equivalent job opportunities in the same locales.

• Recognize the value of entrepreneurship in allowing people to follow their individual vocations.

Means and Experiments

1. Maintain the reductions in individual tax rates mandated in the 1986 tax reform act as central to mass property rights.

2. Replace the current income tax with a consumption tax. For both economic and cultural reasons, saving is good. Currently, our savings rate is one of the lowest in the industrialized world. One way to provide new incentives to save is by replacing the income tax with a consumption tax. We do not envision a value-added tax or anything like it. Rather, an individual would calculate his taxable income exactly as he does now but would deduct any net savings, which would not be subject to taxation. Any net dis-savings—that is, money withdrawn from savings and used for consumption—would be added to taxable income. In effect, a consumption tax simply establishes an unlimited IRA: an IRA to which a person may contribute an unlimited amount, and from which he may draw regardless of age. As with the IRA, contributions are deductible, but withdrawals are taxed. The huge popularity of IRAs during the brief time when they were generally available suggests that replacing the income tax with a consumption tax might be highly effective in reorienting people away from consumption and toward increased saving.

3. Strengthen and expand efforts to reduce regulatory red tape, especially as it applies to new or small-scale entrepreneurs.

4. Pass a Federal Red Tape Compensation act, whereby all government-mandated paperwork would have a rating, reflecting the time that it would reasonably be expected to take to prepare it. The person or firm required to submit the paperwork would be compensated financially according to the rating, with the funds coming from the budget of the agency requiring the work.

5. Expand employee ownership plans as a means of uniting labor and management. State revolving funds, with initial Federal funding (as discussed in the introduction), should be established to enable employees, espe-

cially those of failing companies or facilities slated for closure, to purchase their workplaces.

6. Provide employer tax breaks for employee stock ownership plans.

7. Establish state revolving funds oriented toward community preservation in situations where the existence of the community is endangered by plant closings (see section on community preservation).

8. Encourage the establishment of sabbatical plans in all lines of work, possibly with the stipulation that the sabbatical be used for study or experimentation related to the work.

9. In general, cultural conservatives are strong supporters of free trade, because it tends to benefit all of us as consumers. However, many consumers are also workers, who are threatened by the loss of jobs in certain sectors, and all of us are citizens, whose national security can be diminished by the loss of critical industries. Therefore, we should keep a full range of options in trade policy, including the possibility that, in the case of industries being forced rapidly toward extinction by foreign competition, tariff protection be granted for a limited, non-extendable number of years during which labor and management can cooperatively restructure their operations so as to become competitive. Any such program would depend entirely on the period of protection being short-term and non-extendable. Should protection be long-term, not only would the economic effects be undesirable, but the impetus toward a new institutional culture reflecting the principle of fraternity and cooperation between management and labor would also be lost.

10. Management and ownership that has no interest in the long-term future of the company, and therefore in the workers who depend upon it for employment, is a growing economic problem. To help correct it, stock-

holders should insist that management be compensated according to the company's performance. Some of the compensation should be deferred in such a manner as to depend upon long-term performance; e.g. much of a top executive's salary should be paid in stock, not cash. Golden parachutes and similar management protections should be eliminated, in order to tie management to the company. Government has a clear role to play here in advocacy, and also possibly in taxation of such counter-productive benefits as golden parachutes.

11. In order to help those on welfare move toward independence, welfare should normally include a work requirement for those who are not disabled. The focus of the requirement should not be "punishing" people for being on welfare, but introducing them to the satisfaction that comes from work, the self-respect and the independence it brings.

12. Establish re-training IRAs, to permit workers to save resources directed specifically toward aiding them in making mid-life career transitions.

13. Consider means for insuring long-term currency stability, including but not limited to a return to the gold standard. A "market basket standard" is one possible option.

14. Make permanent the Research and Development (R&D) Tax Credit, and make it applicable to software and start-up companies. As the Heritage Foundation states:

> The Economic Recovery Act of 1981 granted a 25 percent tax credit in research and development expenditures. This has triggered increased R&D investments. However, the credit effectively excludes start-up companies and computer software. Further, the credit expires at the end of 1985 . . . The credit should be made permanent and applied to start-up companies and computer software.[7]

We endorse this proposal, which would be of particular assistance to entrepreneurs.

15. Businesses establishing themselves in Federally designated high unemployment zones should be exempt from the capital gains tax.

NOTES

1. Cf. Alice M. Rivlin, ed., *Economic Choices 1984* (Washington, D.C.: Brookings Institution, 1984), p. 2.

2. "I know of no country, indeed, where the love of money has taken stronger hold on the affections of men and where a profounder contempt is expressed for the theory of the permanent equality of property," says Alexis de Tocqueville, *Democracy in America,* Part I (1835), c. 3; cf. Part II (1840), Book Three, c. 17.

3. Instead we look at the causal influence of deeper cultural factors in making a growing economy possible. The importance of internal moral strengths has already been stressed in the Introduction. But the "work ethic" and the disposition to postpone gratification are not the only keys to economic success.

4. The appreciation of work and enterprise (which are the same: we draw no ideological distinction between a "workers' ethos" and an entrepreneurial one) entered the Western mind primarily through the Bible. The pagans viewed work as a curse, whereas St. Paul demanded gainful employment as a part of the Christian ideal (cf. I Thess. 4:11–12; 2 Thess. 3:10–12); Aristotle discussed many virtues, but none of them quite seems to capture the enterprising spirit of the "virtuous woman" portrayed in Proverbs 31.

5. Here we depart significantly from the view of Adam Smith. In Book IV, chapter 5 of *The Wealth of Nations*, Smith says: "The natural effort of every individual to better his own condition, when suffered to exert itself with freedom and security, is so powerful a principle, that it is alone, and without

any assistance, not only capable of carrying on the society to wealth and prosperity, but of surmounting a hundred impertinent obstructions with which the folly of human laws too often encumbers its operation." Here Smith is making a causal claim. He says that growing prosperity and freedom have as their sufficient condition a definite causal factor made up of two components: (1) individual effort at self-improvement and (2) an initial environment of freedom/security for this effort to operate in. Unlike the French rationalists, Smith did not believe in "natural freedom"; he realized that his second component was a delicate historical and cultural product. But he did believe that his first component, "the effort of every individual to better his own condition," was natural. We disagree. The very idea that betterment is possible, that one's individual betterment vis-à-vis the group is either possible or desirable, and that "effort" (i.e. self-directed work) is a good because it will make betterment possible (or is a good for any other reason)—these, too, are delicate products of a favorable history and culture.

When one recognizes that Smith's "effort" is not natural, one can accept his causal claim and, precisely in so doing, reach the conclusion that the foundation of economic growth is not self-interest but the cultural consensus that sustains "effort" (and its environment of secure freedom).

In just the same way, we depart from John Stuart Mill and a long line of economic rationalists. These thinkers begin their account of economic laws by positing in each agent a calculative rationality by which the agent is able to "reckon" where his interest lies and maximize or "optimalize" his well-being. Such a rationality is deemed "natural" to man, and social-contract theorists have even used it to explain how individuals might have bargained themselves out of the "state of nature." Again, we have no intention of denying that some such form of rationality is crucial to economic theory, but we see nothing "natural" about it. Men have lived in tribal solidarities for millennia without ever imagining the form of thought which Mill attributed to *homo oeconomicus*.

6. As human cameraderie does not exclude competition on

the playing field, so fraternity does not exclude competition in economic life. Competition within a framework of law and civility is a form of cooperation (paradoxical as that may sound), not a form of conflict.

7. Stuart M. Butler, Michael Sanera, and W. Bruce Weinrod, eds., *Mandate for Leadership II* (Washington, D.C.: The Heritage Foundation, 1984), p. 44.

Welfare

To help the less fortunate is one of our country's noblest endeavors. To abandon the poor would be to demean ourselves; but to help the poor without giving them a real chance to escape poverty is to degrade us all.

—Carl A. Anderson[1]

To many people, the conservative position on welfare is simple: we are against it. We simply don't want to spend the money. Just as liberals are seen as being anti-defense, conservatives are viewed as anti-welfare. And some conservatives *are* against welfare. In their view, if a free economy leaves some people destitute—so be it.

The cultural conservative view is different. We accept the obligation to the less fortunate that welfare represents. We accept it because it is one of the West's longest-standing traditions; help for the poor, the sick, the crippled, the widowed and the orphaned is mandated in the Old Testament, our culture's oldest code. We also accept the obligation on functional grounds. To the degree we can help others to become productive, contributing members of society, we help society as a whole. And to the extent we build a system to help those who cannot help themselves, such as the ill and the handicapped, we know the system is there for us and our family, should we ever need it. Even many of those who resent the expense of welfare want a functional "safety net," just in case.

Not only do cultural conservatives accept an obligation toward the less fortunate, we believe it goes beyond providing the bare means of living. It also means helping those who can be helped to free themselves from dependency on welfare. We want to assist people to move out of poverty and into the productive mainstream. The test of every benefit must be this: does it offer the poor a real chance of escape from welfare?

Applying this test helps to reveal important differences among the poor. For some people there simply is no escape; they will always be dependent on support from others, through no fault of their own. Those with severe physical or mental handicaps, the chronically ill or severely injured, and the elderly and infirm are simply not capable of providing for themselves. Cultural conservatives accept the need to provide for them, and to provide not only money but personal involvement as well. We do not fulfill our traditional obligations if we leave the bedridden and the house-bound fed and clothed but also alone and abandoned. We need to provide companionship, stimulation, diversion—the things that make life worth living.

Here, mediating institutions prove that they are irreplaceable. Families, churches, service organizations, and community groups can provide the non-material support that people need far better than can government, because they work through volunteers, through people who have made a personal commitment. Public policy's proper role is to encourage and support mediating institutions in filling this vital need. That may mean contracting out to such institutions, including churches and synagogues, the delivery of government-funded services.

Because those who have no chance of escape make up

a special category of the poor, and because existing
welfare programs often limit the involvement of mediating institutions, it would make sense to amend state and
Federal welfare laws to give these people a special status.
Programs for them should not even be called "welfare"
but, quite simply, humanitarian aid. Cultural conservatives prefer to reserve the term 'welfare' for those who
can escape. This is in keeping with our national consensus that welfare is not something in which we seek to
"maintain" people; it is something we want and expect
people to escape.

A second category of the poor, and statistically the
largest, consists of those who can and *do* escape from
poverty, given only short-term welfare assistance. These
are often intact families, caught in a time of misfortune,
or recently divorced women with dependent children.[2]
For them, the "safety net" seems to be adequate as it
now stands.

The greatest challenge we face is in a third category.
It is the growing "underclass" of able-bodied adults and
their children who persist in long-term patterns of welfare dependency. This class has appeared over the past
twenty years—roughly since the beginning of the "Great
Society" approach to welfare.[3]

This permanent underclass, with disproportionate
black and Hispanic components, has become a fixture in
most of our cities. It is a double curse: to those who are
trapped in it and to those who live near it. It is riddled
with crime, alcoholism and drugs; it is a major cause of
urban blight; it is a severe drain on local economies and
services; and its very existence stands as irrefutable
evidence of national decay and decline. We have had
poor people and poor sections of our cities before, but
this is something new and different.

The difference is culture. Among the new underclass,

functional culture—national and ethnic—has collapsed. It has been replaced with a culture of instant sensual gratification, often through sex, drugs, or alcohol. Traditional prohibitions against these have collapsed, as have moral strictures against crime, including murder.[4] Traditional institutions, including the family, the neighborhood, the church and the school have lost their holds, especially on young people. Most black births are now out of wedlock, teen pregnancy and abortion are common, and males are left unemployed and outside any family structure, which is to say, functionless and irrelevant. That is tragic and dangerous.

From the culturally conservative perspective, this situation is intolerable. It must be corrected. To correct it, we must move beyond dollar welfare to a new concept: cultural welfare.

What is cultural welfare? It is a recognition that the underclass can only be transformed into a normal, productive part of society by transforming its culture. Its dysfunctional values must be replaced by functional values, that is, by traditional values: delayed gratification, work and saving, commitment to family and to the next generation, education and training, self-improvement, and rejection of crime, drugs, and casual sex.

The current welfare system, which is geared merely to providing money, has demonstrated it cannot do the job. Indeed, it has done a great deal—inadvertently—to undermine traditional culture. Aid to Dependent Children is an example. Its intent is laudable, but its results are deplorable. It has spurred the breakdown of the black family, because it is available to never-married women with children. Under cultural welfare, subsidies must be structured to uphold and reward traditional values, not undermine them.

Nor can government do the whole job. Mediating

institutions are vital. Churches in particular must play a central role because of their traditional strength in the black and Hispanic communities. Government should find ways to contract out the delivery of welfare services to churches that take on the task of reviving traditional values in underclass communities. The contracts should be written so as to safeguard the freedom and integrity of the churches' internal discipline and doctrine.

The task of eliminating the underclass and integrating its members into mainstream society is one of the most important and most challenging facing our society. It must be accomplished. The alternative is growing division into two alien nations, each hostile to the other. That is simply not acceptable. We must remain one nation, indivisible.

Goals

• Reduce and eliminate the permanent underclass by integrating its members into the cultural and economic mainstream of American society.

• Build a consensus that this can only be done by addressing the cultural problem: the dysfunctional culture of the underclass. Its dysfunctional values must be replaced with functional, traditional values, with special emphasis on delayed gratification, family, education, work and abstinence from crime, extra-marital sex and drugs.

• Replace dollar welfare with cultural welfare: the close integration of financial subsidies with encouragement of and adherence to traditional values.

Means and Experiments

1. We propose a social compact with the leaders of the black and Hispanic communities. As conservatives,

we will support all the funding necessary for an effective cultural welfare program as an alternative to mere dollar welfare. Instead of leading the fight against welfare, conservatives will help lead the fight for it. We will make cultural welfare our top priority in the competition for Federal funds, equal in our view to defense.

In turn, black and Hispanic leaders will join with us in developing and advocating cultural welfare. They will help devise programs that will combine the financial support welfare recipients require with restoration of functional, traditional values. Black and Hispanic leaders will work to replace current welfare programs with cultural welfare, both in their local communities and on the national level.

2. In cases where black and Hispanic community leaders will not join in such a social compact, we will seek to identify alternate leaders. We recognize that such alternate leaders must come from and be supported by their communities; we cannot and do not propose to attempt to "create" them. But it is clear that cultural breakdown is a growing cause of concern in the black and Hispanic communities, and leaders who share that concern are emerging in those communities. We believe we have something of value to offer to them and look forward to working with them.

3. Adopt a "tough love" approach to welfare. "Tough love" is a program which encourages parents to discipline children who are using drugs. Similar discipline could be helpful in promoting cultural welfare. For example:

    a) We could set a date by which no one who has not graduated from high school could be eligible for any form of Federal welfare, unless they were physically or mentally disabled. Graduation would require passing tough competency tests. Such a program would have to be "grand-fathered," so as not to apply to older individuals. But if those in school knew that they would have to graduate to qualify for welfare, there would be a powerful new impetus behind education.

b) Similarly, after a certain date, cash benefits could be provided only to intact families. Again, this would have to be "grandfathered." But after a certain date, the rule for new applicants could be: if there is no intact family, there will be no federally funded cash benefits. (At the same time, no one would starve or become homeless, because foodstamps and housing benefits, which are non-cash, would remain in place.) Meanwhile, other welfare payments could become available, on a matching grants basis, to any head of an intact family with a full-time job whose income from work was below a certain level.

c) Those under 21 should be excluded from receiving any benefits unless they live with one or both parents.

4. Currently, welfare policy is largely controlled by institutions that represent the providers of welfare, especially the government bureaucracies involved. Often, this leads to policies that benefit the providers much more than the intended recipients, the needy. Federal welfare policy should be altered to attempt to weaken the provider-led coalitions, whose incentive is to increase costs without improving services, and strengthen recipient-led coalitions that are sensitive to the interests of those in need. Two specific means toward this end would be:

a. In awarding Federal funds, rules governing the

credentials of service providers should be liberalized to permit volunteer groups and community organizations, including churches, to qualify as distributors of the services, ending the monopoly of the professional welfare bureaucracies.[5]

b. Renewal of contracts to service providers and renewal of grants to public welfare agencies should both be based on their success record in empowering people to move from welfare-dependency to self-support. As an incentive to success, government could offer early retirement or other suitable benefits to those welfare case-workers who help a set number of households to achieve long-term self-sufficiency.

5. Public housing should move toward home ownership and control by residents. To those ends:

a. The U.S. Department of Housing and Urban Development (HUD) should require Public Housing Authorities to adopt HUD-designed tenant management programs as a condition for receiving Federal operating subsidies and modernization funds; and

b. Congress should pass a "right-to-buy" law, modelled on the British program, which would assist public housing residents to buy and own their own residences. Such a program would empower low-income urban residents to take control of an important part of their lives, while at the same time reducing long-term demands for government funding.[6]

6. Through state revolving funds, offer government financial support to volunteer efforts now underway in some cities to build low-cost inner-city housing for sale rather than rent. The construction effort itself should

remain volunteer; the government should support the mediating institutions that have generated the programs, not take over from them. Government support should again be tied to reinforcement of the family structure, in that government funds should be available only to provide homes for families.

7. Establish state revolving venture capital funds to assist poor families to set up small family businesses. Ideally, much of the funding could be raised privately, perhaps with the revolving fund providing loan guarantees.

8. Establish a program of education vouchers for children from poverty-level households. The poor quality of many inner-city public schools—especially in regard to discipline and learning environment—is a major force in driving young people into the permanent underclass. Education vouchers would facilitate the establishment of alternative, high-quality inner-city schools, characterized by strong discipline.

9. Establish inner-city enterprise zones, with government subsidies for firms locating in such zones who hire poverty-level male heads of household. Firms would be permitted to pay a competitive sub-minimum wage from company funds, with government subsidy added to raise wages for male heads of household to a "family wage" level—the level necessary to support a family. The object would be not merely to bring jobs to the inner city, but to rebuild the functional role of underclass males as heads of households and family providers. Ceding of certain federal taxation rights to the states should be considered as a means to fund this program.

10. Reconsider the policy of de-institutionalizing the mentally ill. While it is generally desirable to de-institutionalize those who can lead independent lives, the widespread de-institutionalization of recent years has put

many people on the streets—literally—who cannot care for themselves. As "street people," their basic needs of food and shelter are often not met. De-institutionalization must be driven by careful consideration of the best interests of the individuals involved, not the desire of governments to reduce the cost of their care.

NOTES

1. White House Briefing, February 9, 1987. Mr. Anderson is Special Assistant to the President for Public Liaison.

2. Michael Novak et al., *The New Consensus on Family and Welfare* (Washington, D.C.: American Enterprise Institute, 1987), p. 45.

3. Proof of the coincidence and, indeed, the causal connection between the spread of the underclass and the taking-hold of Great Society policies is furnished by Charles Murray's remarkable study, *Losing Ground* (New York: Basic Books, 1984). Although many aspects of Murray's case have been attacked by critics, his rebuttals have been generally acknowledged as successful. See Robert Royal, "Charles Murray and His Critics," in Michael Cromartie, ed., *Gaining Ground, New Approaches to Poverty and Dependency* (Washington, D.C.: Ethics and Public Policy Center, 1985), pp. 24–36; see also the Fall 1985 issue of *Political Science Quarterly*.

4. These are descriptive statements; they are not an exercise in "blaming the victim." We do not suggest that the disempowering culture of the underclass is "native" to its members or that it came out of nowhere. On the contrary, much of it has "formed" in recent decades. The tragedy is that it has not only been discrimination or joblessness that have helped to form this culture but also perverse incentives from the public sector.

5. See Stuart M. Butler, *Privatising Federal Spending: A Strategy to Eliminate the Deficit* (New York: Universe Books, 1985), pp. 113–114.

6. *Ibid.*, pp. 70–75.

Conservation and Environment

To waste, to destroy, our natural resources, to skin and exhaust the land instead of using it so as to increase its usefulness, will result in undermining in the days of our children the very prosperity which we ought by right to hand down to them amplified and developed.

—Theodore Roosevelt[1]

Cultural conservatives realize that the words conservative and conservation come from the same root. Just as we strive to conserve the culture, we also seek to conserve the environment and natural resources. Our responsibility to future generations includes leaving them clean air and water, good farmland, living forests, and wilderness areas for recreation. An attitude of "trash it up and move on" is not consistent with culturally conservative beliefs about stewardship, personal responsibility and self-discipline. We are also environmentalists.

At the same time, we see some problems in the environmental movement. Cultural radicalism has had an unfortunate effect upon the environmental movement, pushing segments of it to more and more extreme positions. Some elements of the movement repudiate all willingness to balance human needs with environmental

needs. Human needs are rejected as the incessant demands of an already over-dominant species. Over-popu-
lation and pollution are seen as inherent "contradic-
tions" of capitalism.

More deeply, cultural radicals and the environmentalists whom they have influenced seem to believe that the
risks inherent in human fallibility can be escaped. They
argue that if we convert to an anti-technological culture,
we will stop making mistakes. We can achieve salvation
by overthrowing Western culture and making nature our
god.[2]

The evidence of history is different. The environmental disasters of the past were not products of Western
man alone but happened all over the world, and from the
dawn of history, as ordinary results of natural phenomena and human fallibility. Most of the species that have
disappeared (more than 90% of those that ever existed
are gone) are thought by scientists to have disappeared
with no help whatever from mankind.

But each group of humans did its share also. The
cavemen hunted the mammoth to extinction along with
dozens of other species. Early agriculture ruined the soil
with slash and burn methods. Palestine was deforested
in the early Bronze Age, and so was the Ganges valley.
American Indians nearly wiped out the buffalo before
white men killed any.[3] The state-managed irrigation systems of Mesopotamia and China were as prone to environmental disaster as are the state-managed resources of
Soviet Russia.

Neither nature-cults nor "low" technology protect
nature. Socialism does not protect nature. Resources are
protected by human beings who have the incentive, the
knowledge, and the affluence to do so. It is traditional
Western culture that produces such human beings. The

tidy farms, villages and forests of Western Europe were a model of land management.

Admittedly, modern society brings special challenges. The technological dynamism of the Western world brings a steady stream of new industries and, with them, new wastes, whose impact on the environment is initially unknown or even unknowable. As companies compete, energy needs rise, and populations increase, demands on the environment grow. As they grow, the ozone seems to slip away from us and some rains turn to acid. A "greenhouse effect" threatens the world's climate. Have these challenges become unmanageable?

Cultural conservatives say no. We side with those environmentalists who prefer constructive action over despair or cultural revolution. In fact, we believe that a coalition is possible between constructive, common-sense environmentalists, among whom we count ourselves, and the millions of ordinary Americans who owe their jobs and future hopes to a growing industrial economy.

The coalition can start with the premise that knowledge and innovation are essential to both kinds of advance—environmental and industrial. For example, research into insect-resistant strains of popular vegetables not only promises a better bargain at the grocery counter but could also eliminate pesticides from millions of acres of farmland. Similar progress on a cotton plant that tastes bad to boll weevils would drastically reduce the use of pollutant chemicals across the South; environmentalists could rejoice, while millions of ordinary Americans applauded in cheaper shorts.[4]

The coalition can then agree on the preconditions for expanded knowledge and effective innovation. Good research must be conducted and updated continually, if the impact of new processes and their wastes are to be understood, and if corrective measures are to be applied. The corrective measures themselves need to be tested. So progress—economic and environmental—means more science, not less. It does not come from hugging trees, but from holding polluters accountable and encouraging constructive innovation.

And progress requires a certain kind of society—a society affluent enough to set aside major investments for basic and applied science and for retooling of industrial processes. Poor and stagnant economies cannot afford these things. Prosperity and growth, far from being threats to the environment, are necessary preconditions for environmentalism.

If better ideas are not simply to gather dust, but are to be used, then progress requires broad diffusion throughout society of the *incentive* to apply those ideas to improve the environment. This is why the new coalition will turn away from bureaucratic solutions. This is not a matter of ideology, but of the demonstrated fact that bureaucracies do not perform well. They bring centralized planning and decision-making, which are notoriously uncreative.

This is as true in environmental policy as it is elsewhere. The Nuclear Regulatory Commission manages on the one hand to hamstring nuclear power plants while, on the other, it fails to prevent a virtually constant (though thus far mercifully minor) stream of accidents in the facilities it permits to operate. The draconian Clean Air amendments of 1970 imposed enormous costs of compliance on certain industries but gave them no incentive to comply. Instead, it gave them an incentive to achieve delays through politically brokered compromises. Too often, detailed regulation and bureaucratic solutions stifle the industries on which ordinary Americans depend and yet do not provide environmentalists with the good results they seek. This is true even in wilderness and park areas. As Alston Chase has demonstrated, the National Park Service fundamentally misunderstands the needs of our national parks and the type of management they require.[5] The "Superfund" for cleanup of toxic wastes has become little more than a political pork barrel.

The new coalition will seek ways to address environmental problems that rely heavily on private initiatives and incentives, with the freedom of innovation they imply. The Carter administration undertook one significant initiative in this direction when it moved toward tradable emission permits as a partial replacement for bureaucratic specification of industrial technologies and procedures. Such permits work to restore incentive—to enhance effective and efficient control measures by private parties. Regrettably, the Reagan administration EPA has limited such permits to old facilities.

The new coalition will also recognize that government's role in dealing with environmental problems has much to do with establishing accountability. This must often be done by establishing clear property rights. The buffalo would not have been hunted to the brink of extinction if property rights to lands and herds had existed on the wild frontier. Establishing property rights can supplement other roles of government, such as writing laws against activities that are clearly beyond the pale, providing policing, using the "pulpit" and force of example to encourage environmentally sound behavior, and holding people personally responsible for the results of their polluting and other environmentally damaging actions. By combining personal liability with the profit motive, government can move private industry toward environmentally sound practices without relying on centralized, bureaucratic control.

Cultural conservatives should lead the effort to form this new coalition and, through it, to develop an environmentalism that is both effective and consistent with society's need for growth and progress.

Goals

• Develop a new coalition between environmentalists and American workers and businessmen whose livelihoods depend on prosperity, economic growth and technological progress.

• Make economic growth and conservation of the environment and natural resources march hand-in-hand, rather than seeming to oppose one another. Far from being contradictory, environmentalism depends on prosperity; only a growing and prosperous society has sufficient wherewithal to fund protection of the environment.

• Adopt "common sense environmentalism." Development is inevitable and necessary, but it can be channeled so as to preserve the environment through forcing accountability and encouraging constructive innovation.

• Encourage longer-term thinking in regard to resources. We have a responsibility to future generations to be good stewards of the resources on which they, like us, may depend.

Means and Experiments

It is useful to look at specific means and experiments in two categories, private and governmental.

Private

1. Encourage individuals to participate in the new environmental coalition by influencing the policy of corporations in which they hold stock. Many companies

already follow environmentally sound policies. But too many do not. Culturally conservative shareholders should take the lead in demanding sound, common-sense environmentalism from their corporations. One example of an issue they can raise is the desirability of revising industrial and resource-related processes, rather than simply adding anti-pollution or resource conserving devices to existing processes. Add-ons are usually less efficient economically as well as environmentally than process revision; e.g. it is often both better and cheaper to produce less toxic waste in an industrial process than to focus solely on storing waste more safely.

2. Following the constructive precedent set by the Audubon Society, which manages the Rainey Refuge in Louisiana and other lands in Michigan, environmental activist groups should seek to acquire (including from the Federal government) management rights or property rights over ecologically sensitive areas. Then *they* could make the decisions regarding use and abuse.

Governmental

1. Government can and must help protect individuals against risks imposed against their will by others. One way to do this would be to require surety bonds where potentially dangerous technologies or toxic wastes are involved. A corporation or individual would have to post a perpetual bond, of an amount proportional to the risk involved, the principal of which would be taken to repair any environmental damage the owner inflicted. If the owner inflicted no such damage, he would continue to receive interest on the bond as income.[6]

2. Congress should take steps to set up Wilderness Endowment Boards to manage existing wilderness areas as Trusts for the public. Board members would be selected by a joint committee of Congress from nominees

proposed by respected environmental and conservation groups, and their single goal would be to protect and enhance wilderness values. Somewhat similar to the trustees of a college endowment, the board would be free to add to or subtract from existing wilderness holdings, to set standards for development, and to sell or withhold development rights, so long as these actions carried out the board's legal responsibility to enhance wilderness values. Board actions would be subject to Congressional veto.[7]

3. When corporations pollute, citizens must be protected against uncompensated invasions of clean air, water or land. New Jersey offers an example of how this can be done. There, local governments have an option to accept or reject power plants. Those who would build such plants must first work out a compensation scheme acceptable to one of the localities. Then the residents of that locality are compensated for somewhat dirtier air by a reduction in their property taxes. Because a cleaner plant can secure a permit to operate with smaller compensatory payments, power companies have an incentive to build cleaner plants and to control their pollution effectively.

4. The concept of tradable emission permits, introduced by the Carter administration, should be expanded. Princeton University economics professor Alan S. Blinder describes one way this might be done: by expanding the EPA's "bubble" program. He writes.

> Under the bubble concept, all sources of pollution from a single plant or firm are imagined to be encased in a mythical bubble. The EPA tells the company how much it may emit into the bubble, but lets the company decide how to comply . . . A bubble is essentially an emissions permit that is not bought and may not be sold. Hence it is

but a small step from bubbles to marketable emissions permits . . .[8]

Marketable permits, in addition to strengthening incentives to reduce pollution, would also raise revenue for the government—possibly billions of dollars of revenue.

5. Through education and providing information, government could encourage further development of "soft energy." Soft energy is local and individual conservation, coupled with local energy sources, such as methane from waste disposal, local hydro power, and wind and solar energy for the home. Soft energy not only reduces demand for non-renewable energy sources; it also decentralizes energy production, which reduces national vulnerability to energy shortages. Power companies could also encourage soft-energy development. They could alter their rate structures to confront power users with the true cost of using additional power, without changing total power bills in the short run, yet saving users big money over time, as soft energy use expanded.

6. Government should support vigorous research into potential environmental disasters such as depletion of the ozone layer and the "greenhouse effect." Such research is a *sine qua non* for intelligent policy making.

7. Strong support should also be given to research into nuclear fusion. Fusion potentially offers an answer to the serious problem of nuclear wastes posed by nuclear fission power plants.

8. Apply the "sodbuster" concept to all erodible land. Under this concept, no one who brings erodible land into agricultural production may qualify for any form of agricultural assistance. As the Heritage Foundation noted in proposing this conservation measure, "Such a policy would make the farm programs consistent with a conservation effort and would establish an Administration pol-

icy of discouraging poor farming practices that contribute to soil erosion."[9]

9. The Environmental Protection Agency should explore the feasibility of introducing harmless tracer elements into plant waste outflows. This could assist materially in determining responsibility for water and ground pollution.[10]

NOTES

1. Message to Congress, December 3, 1907.

2. For an excellent discussion of culturally radical environmentalism, see Alston Chase, "The Great, Green Deep-Ecology Revolution," *Rolling Stone,* April 23, 1987, p. 61.

3. See John Baden, Richard Stroup, and Walter Thurman, "Myths, Admonitions and Rationality: The American Indian as a Resource Manager," *Economic Inquiry* 19 (1981), 132–143.

4. Research of this kind is being done at the Monsanto Company. See the *Wall Street Journal,* July 21, 1987, p. 31.

5. Alston Chase, *Playing God in Yellowstone: The Destruction of America's First National Park* (Atlantic Monthly Press, 1986).

6. We are indebted to Richard Stroup of the Political Economy Research Center for this idea and the two following.

7. For a full exposition of this idea, see Richard L. Stroup and John Baden, "Endowment Areas: A Clearing in the Policy Wilderness?" *Cato Journal* 2 (Winter, 1982), 691–708; a shorter account has appeared in *Forest Planning,* June, 1985.

8. Alan S. Blinder, "Why Not Sell Pollution by the Pound?" *The Washington Post,* August 18, 1987, p. A 15. It should be noted, however, that getting the full benefit of this approach will require amending the definitions of 'source' and 'facility' in the Clean Air Act.

9. Stuart M. Butler, Michael Sanera, and W. Bruce Wein-

rod, edd., *Mandate for Leadership II: Continuing the Conservative Revolution* (Washington, D.C.: The Heritage Foundation, 1984), p. 21.

10. *Ibid.*, p. 88.

Religious and Moral Institutions

If he be an unbeliever, he will be too profound and large-minded to ridicule religion or to act against it; he is too wise to be a dogmatist or a fanatic in his infidelity. He respects piety and devotion; he even supports institutions as venerable, beautiful, or useful, to which he does not assent; he honors the ministers of religion, and it contents him to decline its mysteries without assailing or denouncing them.

—John Henry Newman[1]

Public policy does not exist in a vacuum. It exists in a cultural environment, in which actions tend to reflect the culture's moral premises. For example, policies toward the homeless reflect our culture's view of the unfortunate; we see them as human beings who deserve our concern, rather than sub-human outcasts or objects of contempt. That perception is rooted in our morality.

Almost always, a culture and its morality have a religion behind them, whose influence lingers on even if the religion is no longer believed, or no longer invoked in public debate. It remains the original source of the values the culture reflects. That fact does not automatically mean the religion is still important. It may be a matter of

101

mere curiosity to historians of ideas, if the religion itself has been dead for centuries.

On the other hand, if the religion is still widely believed, it has continuing importance as a source of values—values which affect people's behavior, and therefore affect the nation. In such a case, there is a real, functional, empirically observable relationship between religion and public policy.

This fact offers a new basis for approaching the difficult matter of religion and public policy in the United States, because it points to a fundamental difference between "church and state" and "religion and public policy." The question of church and state is whether the state should profess a specific religious belief. The question of religion and public policy is whether the goals of the nation are affected by changes in religious demographics (changes in belief, degree of observance, etc.). If policies to which the government has committed itself are significantly affected, in their chances of success, by religious variables, then it is irrational on purely secular grounds for policy-makers to ignore those variables. In such a case, the task we face is to find constitutionally permissible ways to address religious factors.

Framed this way, the question of religion and public policy is not loaded. It does not suggest that demographic changes in religion always affect the odds of success of public policies. If, in a specific case, the rise or decline of religious observance does not affect the odds, then in that case there is no issue of religion and public policy.

If, on the other hand, religion does affect the results of policy, then it should be taken into account, as any other factor would be. The framework itself is neutral.

This neutrality is itself a change, in that until recently it was often assumed that religion was not a serious social force. A reductionist theory—with both capitalist and Marxist variations—held that any measurable difference in social policy outcomes attributed to religion could in fact be explained in more fundamental economic terms. Religion was peripheral and was anyway assumed to be in decline. The further growth of prosperity would soon see it wither away. Twenty years ago, even theologians were often resigned to this point of view. Like Harvey Cox, they anticipated the coming of a "secular city" and wrestled with the meaning of their faith in such a future.

But that future never came. The Bhagwan came, as did a swarm of other gurus. The rebellious youth of the '60s wandered into a myriad of mystical cults. The Moral Majority arose to baffle the pollsters, and much of black America passed the mantle of Dr. King to the shoulders of the Rev. Jesse Jackson without ever finding a secular voice. The Ayatollah's Iran has certainly confounded all secular predictions. In fact, it has become so obvious that religious movements are able on their own to change the balance of social forces that Marxist insurgents now use what their theory condemns by supporting People's Churches and liberation theologies.

The economic reductionist view has failed; it simply does not accord with the facts. Clearly, religious belief can be and often is a social force, with objective effects on society's behavior. Our framework permits us to acknowledge this—to let religion be a consideration in public policy, when in fact it affects public behavior.

Within this framework, where do cultural conservatives stand? Our position is pro-religious. We believe religion makes a massive and positive contribution to the well-being of our society.

The historical evidence is overwhelming; religious belief has played a major role in making us a free and prosperous people.[2] Current statistical evidence shows it continues to play a large and positive role. When religious belief is measured by plausible tests of its intensity (daily prayer, Bible reading, and frequent attendance, weekly or more often, at services), the most religious fifth of the population scores enormously better than the least religious fifth in such areas as frequency of drug abuse, commission of minor crimes, attempted suicides, teenage pregnancy rates, job retention, and voter turnout.[3] There is no real doubt that certain national policies, such as the containment of AFDC costs, will have a better chance of success in proportion to the thriving of religion.

However, in saying that cultural conservatives are pro-religious, there is risk of a fatal misinterpretation. The American consensus around freedom and prosperity supplies for us the criterion by which we look at the features of various cultures, including our own; we seek what contributes to these values and to their long endurance. We are not romantic nationalists, touting our culture's traditional religion for no better reason than that it is "ours," or bashing outsiders for the misfortune of not being "us." We welcome with interest the cultures of all the peoples who have achieved free institutions and economic development. Thus, in turning to the subject of religion, the point of cultural conservatism is not to mandate some "American religion," even if there were such a thing, but to support the contribution which religious beliefs generally make to the stability of our families, the safety of our streets, the morals of our youth, and the honesty of our work-places.[4]

Again, it is not just a reasonable view of the evidence which mandates this stance, but also the collapse of a rival position. The end of the last century and the beginning of this one saw a number of currents of thought converging on the thesis that religion is not just untrue (which many people have held without discounting religion as a social benefit) but also pernicious. These contributory currents included Social Darwinism and Nietzschean humanism as well as the more familiar movements of Marx and Freud. What they all had in common was a bitter enmity towards the morality of the West, including even its exhortations to altruism. Such morality was viewed as a counter-evolutionary coddling of the unfit (Sumner), a sniveling "slave morality" (Nietzsche), an alienating "bourgeois" ideology (Marx), or an engine of sexual repression (Freud). Therefore, the religions which taught and enforced this morality (Judaism just as much as Christianity) were evil influences, opiates and worse, from which the world needed to be freed. These views gained a certain dominance among our cultural and educational elites, thanks to their literary transmission through Shaw, Ibsen, Zola, Lawrence, Dreiser, and many others.

The conviction that religion is outmoded, harmful, or otherwise not to be encouraged is still lively among our opinion-makers, but the intellectual sources which once nourished it have dried up. Social Darwinism is extinct as a moral philosophy, and Marxism has become a cruel disappointment. Nietzschean and other forms of atheist existentialism have degenerated into campus postures, and there is much dispute about what is left from the legacy of Freud. These developments do not vindicate religious claims to truth, of course, but they leave the post-Victorian hostility to religion hanging in thin air.

Among those who still harbor resentment toward religion, many do so out of little more than prejudice. Ignoring the thousands of colleges, hospitals, orphanages, soup-kitchens, credit-unions, housing projects, and other charities sustained by religious institutions, they pretend that all religion is a scam, with an Elmer Gantry figure somewhere in the background.[5]

In calling for a new and positive look at religion's social and cultural utility, cultural conservatives appeal to all fair and open-minded persons, including those who decline to affirm a religious belief personally. One's ability or inability to credit religious doctrines should not distort the perception of a social fact: that religion is beneficial on a massive scale.[6]

Our goals, then, are the following.

Goals

• Give religion and traditional morality the respect which they have earned by their works.

• Recognize that a general encouragement of religion does not violate the principle of separation of church and state, which is directed against the establishment by the state of a specific religion.

• Return to our tax-supported institutions, especially state and local governments and public schools, a measure of legal flexibility, so that they can experiment with mutually beneficial partnerships with religious institutions, again on a non-sectarian basis.

Means and Experiments

1. Overturn that aspect of the 1947 *Everson* decision in which the Supreme Court held that any government action which (a) "aids one religion" (even in a non-discriminatory fashion) or (b) "aids all religions" is unconstitutional—just as would be an action which "prefers one religion over another." This aspect of *Everson v. Board of Education* has saddled us with a constitu-

tional interpretation which, instead of limiting itself to the area of church and state, preempts the religion and public policy field. This is not constitutionally sound in terms of original intent, and it is dysfunctional in terms of its effects on public policy. Religion is a fact to be reckoned with in public life, and we need a framework of public law which is open enough to deal with it.[7]

2. Cease placing a financial burden on parents who seek to give their children a religious education—and thus a training in traditional morals. One means of doing this is to offer educational vouchers, redeemable at both public and religious schools. Alternatively, public schools could offer non-sectarian courses in traditional morals and/or make released-time arrangements for students who wish to receive religious instruction from the clergy of their own faith.

3. Churches, synagogues, and other religious and moral institutions located among the poor should be regarded as major sources of talent and expertise on the distribution of welfare benefits. Their role can be enhanced without church-state entanglement by "privatizing" the delivery of welfare (see section on welfare).

4. Federal funds should be withheld from school districts in which the textbooks show a bias against religion or fail to report accurately the contributions of religion to American life, past and present.[8]

5. On the first day of school, students should bring their textbooks home for their parents to examine.

6. Those who adhere to traditional values and morals should not be compelled to provide financial support to cultural radicalism, e.g., compulsory union dues should not be used by a union's national leadership to support culturally radical causes when most of a union's members are culturally conservative.

Notes

1. *The Idea of a University* (1873), from the section entitled, "The Man of the World."

2. A. James Reichley, *Religion in American Public Life* (Washington, D.C.: Brookings Institution, 1985).

3. Richard B. Freeman, "The Relationship of Churchgoing and Other Background Factors to the Socio-economic Performance of Black Male Youths from Inner City Tracts," in Richard B. Freeman and Harry J. Holzer, eds., *The Black Youth Employment Crisis* (Chicago: University of Chicago Press, 1986); Steven Stack, "The Effect of the Decline of Institutionalized Religion on Suicide, 1954-1978," *Journal for the Scientific Study of Religion* 22 (1983) 239-252; Bradley R. Hertel and Michael Hughes, "Religious Affiliation, Attendance, and Support for 'Pro-Family' Issues in the United States," *Social Forces* 65, no. 3 (March, 1987) 858-882; an important clearinghouse for information on the social and behavioral impact of religion is the Family Research Council of America, Inc., 515 2nd Street N.E., Washington, D.C., 20002.

4. Alexis de Tocqueville is categorical: "Liberty cannot be established without morality, nor morality without faith," *Democracy in America* I, 12.

5. The tartufferie of Jim and Tammy Bakker has recently rekindled this prejudice. But if "guilt by association" is intellectually corrupt when practiced against political figures, it is no less corrupt when practiced against religious figures (including televangelists).

6. This is not to deny, of course, that religion is transcendental in its purpose. It does not exist to provide a public benefit in this world, but to bring men into harmony with God and the demands of a higher world. Cultural conservatives acknowledge this purpose, and hence we reject those anthropological theories which forcibly "re-interpret" religion along social-functionalist lines. Such reduction is always a falsification. When we speak of religion's social benefit, we are speaking rather of a spill-over effect, an "externality," if you will.

Theologians have often pointed to the same evidence of benefit, but as an apologetical argument for the truth of their faith.

When cultural conservatives attribute benefits to the generic thing, "religion," rather than to this or that religion, they are enjoying a luxury of Western culture, where almost all of the influential religions have been variants of Judaism or Christianity. In other cultural settings, one could not speak so loosely. In other cultures an influential religion has sometimes been quite destructive. The cultus of the Hummingbird Wizard cost an estimated two million human lives in Aztec Mexico. The ancient Phoenician religions were not pretty either (one remembers Moloch). Few would care to praise the amoral gnostic sect of the Paulicians, the medieval Islamic heresy called the Assassins, or the sect of the thuggees in India.

Cultural conservatives are aware, therefore, that *in the last analysis,* the social benefit of a religion cannot be separated from its theological and moral content, nor from the question of its truth. But the last analysis is not the only analysis, and a shallower level of discussion may be adequate for many public-policy purposes.

7. A magnificent analysis of the constitutional flaws in *Everson* and its sequelae is Justice Rehnquist's dissent in *Wallace v. Jaffree.*

8. Paul Vitz's important study, *Censorship: Evidence of Bias in Our Children's Textbooks* (Ann Arbor: Servant, 1986) has won the assent of People for the American Way and other organizations not noted for sensing a "lack" of religious presence in our society. This development suggests that a workable public consensus on textbook compliance might be attainable.

Crime and Punishment

There is a craziness in our society when you care more
for the rights of those alleged to have committed crime
than you do for the rights of society.

—Mayor Ed Koch

One of government's most basic functions is to protect
its citizens from crime, especially violent crime:
murder, rape, robbery, and assault. Today, American
governments—Federal, state, and local—are failing to
perform this function effectively. Many Americans live
each day in fear of violent crime. This was not true fifty
or even thirty years ago. Nor is it true in other developed
countries.

It is intolerable. Every American, woman or man,
young or old, rich or poor, white, black or Hispanic, has
the right to be able to walk around his neighborhood in
the day or at night, leave his home and car unattended,
go downtown, let his daughter walk home from school
and his small children play outside their yard safely and
without fear.

The issue is not just incidence of crime. It is equally
fear of crime. If many of us must live our lives in constant
fear of crime, our government has failed us in a fundamental matter. As cultural conservatives, we believe that
every citizen has a right to live in an ordered society.

Until we can, our police and judicial systems stand in need of reform.

What are the failings of the current systems? In broad terms, there are three:

First, our police are not sufficiently effective in apprehending criminals and, what is perhaps even more important, in deterring them. Deterrence is in part a result of apprehension, but it is also a result of presence: of having neighborhood police on the streets. Many neighborhoods seldom see a policeman, and when they do, he is isolated in a fast-moving patrol car. He has no personal relationships with the people in the neighborhood, without which his effectiveness is limited.[1]

This is not the fault of the police themselves. In most communities, there are not enough police to provide the "neighborhood cop" who is part of the community in which he walks a regular beat. Further, the police are often hampered in their work by restraints that are unrelated to legitimate rights.

The result—lack of effective policing of many communities—is unacceptable. Citizens have a basic right to police protection.

Second, too many courts have little to do with justice. Justice, to be worthy of the name, must have three parts: justice to the accused, justice to the victim, and justice to the society. The first gets a great deal of attention, which it should. But much of the attention is in the form of insistence on various procedures which have little to do with determining whether he is or is not guilty. As Attorney General Edwin Meese III has said,

> The system of criminal prosecution, trial, and punishment will ultimately be judged unfair—and thus lose both legitimacy and public confidence—when the results it produces bear no relationship to actual guilt or innocence.

This can occur when the innocent are unfairly prosecuted or punished. But it can also happen when the criminal justice system is perceived as wantonly and randomly freeing, or failing to convict or punish, those who have actually committed crimes.[2]

Too often, guilty parties escape conviction through procedural loopholes, judicial niceties that elevate form over substance. It is time the procedures were brought into line with the central function of the court: determining guilt or innocence as accurately as possible.

In most contemporary American courts, the other two aspects of justice—justice to the victim and justice to the society—receive little or no attention.[3] The victim's right to have his tormentor punished carries little weight in the face of theories of social causes for crime—which in effect declare the guilty to be innocent—and a philosophy of "rehabilitate, don't punish" on the part of many judges.[4] Very few recognize the victim's right to see the criminal punished as a return for the suffering he wantonly inflicted on the innocent.

Nor does society get much consideration. Society's right is simple: it has the right to be free from fear of crime. Every society has some crime, but in many countries, violent crime is sufficiently infrequent that people need give the possibility little thought. They live essentially free from fear of crime.

Americans deserve the same freedom. Courts must consider society's right to freedom from fear of crime, especially in sentencing. Ideally, there should be no such thing as third offenders in the case of violent crimes; after two serious offenses, the criminal should in most cases spend the rest of his life sequestered from society.[5] Further, bail and *habeas corpus* should be severely restricted for a person arraigned for a violent crime when a preponderance of evidence shows the person in question committed the crime.[6] As a goal, there should be no habitually violent criminals at large.

The third failure of the present system is punishment. Punishment seldom includes restitution to the victim. Too often, it is a short prison sentence, short in part because of shortages of jail space. While non-violent crime is often punished best by means other than incarceration, violent crime demands incarceration and thus incapacitation—for life, usually without parole, after the second serious offense.[7]

At the same time, even the murderer and the rapist deserve a prison that itself is under the law. Today, many of our prisons are hellholes of gang warfare and homosexual rape. This breeds further contempt for the law in prisoners who will return to society, and subjects all prisoners to what even strict constructionists would agree borders on cruel and unusual punishment. Punishment reform, including prison reform, must be part of our agenda.

What goals can we set, in light of these failures of the present system of crime and punishment?

Goals

• A society largely free not only of violent crime itself, but of fear of violent crime. This freedom must extend to the poor as well as the rich, to the inner city as well as the suburb. In defining what we mean by "largely" free of crime, the incidence of violent crime in Canada would provide a reasonable standard. No United States citizen should need have more fear of violent crime than does a Canadian.

• Each neighborhood should have adequate police protection—adequate to deter crime as well as to apprehend a majority of violent criminals. Adequacy should be determined neighborhood by neighborhood, not on city-wide or larger scales. As long as any single neighborhood lacks effective police protection, the situation is unacceptable and the local jurisdiction must take remedial action.

• Courts must provide justice to *all* parties: the accused, the victim, and the society. Justice to the victim must include restitution by the criminal, to the degree this is possible. Justice for society must include permanently removing habitually violent criminals—those with two convictions—from society.

• Court procedures must facilitate, not interfere with, determining guilt or innocence. Procedures which result in the guilty escaping conviction are not acceptable.

• Sufficient jail space must be provided so that all who are convicted of crimes of violence serve meaningful sentences, including life sentences for virtually all of those guilty of two violent crimes.

• Prisons must maintain good order. There should be no gang rule, homosexual rape, or other crimes in prisons.

• Maximum efforts should be made to engage first offenders in useful, rewarding labor, and to return them to society with the potential to be productive citizens.

Means and Experiments

1. Citizens should urge local authorities to provide neighborhood police in all areas. This may require readjustment of local spending priorities. Effective police protection should be recognized as a top priority in all localities.

2. Many areas, especially older cities, do not have the funds to provide adequate police protection. To pro-

vide a sufficient number of police, states should be encouraged to establish a Police Corps. In effect a police ROTC, a Police Corps would offer full college scholarships in return for three years of service in the state police. While a Police Corps member would receive a modest salary during his service, he would not receive pension and other benefits that drive up the cost of hiring regular police officers. Normally, his service would be in his home area, and would be as a "cop on the beat"— someone patrolling an area on foot.

To support and encourage the formation of state Police Corps, the Federal government should offer to cede an area of taxation—such as a portion of current federal taxes on tobacco or alcohol—to any state establishing such a program.

3. Sentences should normally include restitution to the victims by the criminal, to the degree possible, and community service.

4. Both Federal and state legislation should mandate life sentences for criminals convicted of a second serious, violent crime. Reductions for "good time" should be possible, but exceptional.

5. *Habeas corpus* and bail provisions should be revised with regard to violent criminals. Normally, where a preponderance of evidence of guilt exists, persons arraigned for a violent crime should not be allowed back in society pending trial.

6. The federal government should take the lead to eliminate court procedures which allow the guilty to escape conviction. Court process must be focused on determining guilt or innocence. If necessary, a Constitutional amendment dealing with arrest and court procedures should be passed.

7. The federal government should temporarily aid the states in providing sufficient jail space for all violent

criminals to serve their full sentences. Federal lands in areas with small population should be considered for establishment of large, high security prisons. At the same time, both Federal and state governments should make much more use of sentences other than incarceration for those convicted of non-violent crimes, thus freeing needed jail space.

8. The Federal government should set the example of prison reform in Federal penitentiaries. The military Disciplinary Barracks at Fort Leavenworth, Kansas, a prison well known for its excellent order and discipline, could serve as a model.

9. The Fort Leavenworth Disciplinary Barracks and some foreign prison systems could also serve as models for engaging prisoners in productive labor and thus increasing the chances for individuals to be rehabilitated. Again, the Federal government should make its prisons models for state institutions in this regard.

10. Both in cases of violent crime where bail is allowed and in most cases of non-violent crime, a private, professional bail agent should be used wherever possible to insure that if the defendant fails to appear, he will be tracked and reapprehended.[8]

11. Criminals should not be permitted to pay attorneys with proceeds from their crimes. Courts should interpret forfeiture statutes to include attorney's fees.[9]

12. The insanity defense should be restricted in cases of violent crimes. A verdict of "not guilty by reason of insanity" should not be permitted. Instead, conviction of actual commission of the crime would bring a verdict of "guilty, but insane," with incarceration in an appropriate institution.

13. For first offenders, especially in cases of juvenile crime, alternatives to incarceration should be considered.[10] For relatively minor offenses, a creative option is

to have the guilty party or parties purchase a large advertisement in the local paper, in which they acknowledge their offense and apologize to those victimized.

14. Victims of crimes should be informed as to the sentence given to the person who committed the crime against them. They should have the right to appeal the sentence. Any early parole or clemency should require consideration of the views of the victim.

15. A measure similar to the Federal Sentencing Improvement Act, recently introduced by Senators Armstrong and Nunn, should be passed into law.

NOTES

1. "The first thing to understand," says Jane Jacobs, "is that the public peace—the sidewalk and street peace—of cities is not kept primarily by the police, necessary as police are. It is kept primarily by an intricate, almost unconscious, network of voluntary controls and standards among the people themselves" (*The Death and Life of Great American Cities,* 1961). Our point is that, in order to be effective, the policeman must fit into this network on a real and daily basis. See David A. Jones and L. Stephen Jennings, "The Sidewalk and Street Peace: Safeguarding America's Finest," in Patrick B. McGuigan and Jon S. Pascale, eds., *Crime and Punishment in Modern America* (Washington, D.C.: Free Congress Research and Education Foundation, 1986), pp. 231-258.

2. "Crime and Punishment in Modern America," in McGuigan and Pascale, *op. cit.,* pp. 11-12.

3. See Patrick B. McGuigan and Randall R. Rader, eds., *Criminal Justice Reform* (Washington, D.C.: Free Congress Foundation, 1983).

4. On the weakness of that philosophy, see C. S. Lewis, *The Problem of Pain,* and Russell Kirk, "Criminal Character and Mercy," in McGuigan and Rader, *op. cit.,* pp. 213-223.

5. See Kenneth W. Starr, "The Impetus for Sentencing Reform in the Criminal Justice System," in McGuigan and Pascale, pp. 299-312.

6. Randall R. Rader, "Bailing Out a Failed Law: The Constitution and Pretrial Detention," in McGuigan and Rader, pp. 91-112; William French Smith, "A Proposal for Habeas Corpus Reform," *ibid.*, pp. 137-154.

7. William L. Armstrong and Sam Nunn, "Alternatives to Incarceration: The Sentencing Improvement Act," in McGuigan and Pascale, pp. 337-348.

8. See Gerald P. Monks, "Public Bail—A National Disaster?" *ibid.*, pp. 139-152.

9. Patrick B. McGuigan, "Forfeiture of Attorneys Fees: *Caveat Juris Doctor,*" in *Ibid.*, pp. 153-170.

10. A model program is the Eckerd Youth Development Center in North Okeechobee, Florida, a private facility to which the state of Florida contracts out a portion of its youth corrections program.

Military Reform

You see, it is not conceivable that an American force in Vietnam would meet . . . the sad fate of the French army. It is not a question of bravery but of technology.

—Secretary of Defense Robert S. McNamara, 1962[1]

For many years our national defense debate had only two sides and was rather narrow. Conservatives generally wanted to spend more for defense. Most liberals wanted to spend less. Both were concerned mainly about money and budgeting.

However, the last few years have seen a third party enter the defense debate: the military reform movement. The military reformers are focused not on the size of the defense budget, but on winning in combat. Their main goal is American armed forces that can win if called upon to fight. In their view, more money spent the same way we spend it today will not make our defense problems go away—and might make them worse. More money does not automatically mean more defense. If we want to have effective armed forces, we need to think less about how much to spend and more about what we are spending it for.[2]

The military reform movement has a second goal. The reformers want the support of the nation for a strong defense, not just for one or two years, but for the long

119

haul. They believe the American people will only support the defense the country needs if they are convinced they are getting their money's worth.[3]

Military reform focuses on our conventional forces— the forces most likely to be called upon in a crisis. The reform movement includes many serving military officers, mostly younger officers, along with some civilian defense theorists and some members of Congress. In Congress, the reformers have founded the Military Reform Caucus, which now includes about 130 Senators and Representatives. It is almost evenly divided between Republicans and Democrats. And it is one of the few such groups in Congress that includes both liberals and conservatives. Conservatives active in the Caucus include Representatives Newt Gingrich, Tom Ridge, and Denny Smith and Senator Charles Grassley.

The military reformers believe that although much of the current defense debate is focused on money and equipment, people are most important for winning in combat, ideas are second, and equipment is only third. They have raised a large number of specific issues in each area, including:

• Our military promotion system currently tends to promote bureaucrats, careerists, and courtiers instead of leaders, trainers, tacticians and warriors. If we want to win in combat, we must reverse that practice.

• The services' "up or out" promotion system, under which an officer must be promoted continuously or retire, is wrong. It forces officers to become careerists, and careerism too often means looking good instead of being good.

• Our forces have far too many officers above the company grades. The officer surplus leads to tremendous personnel turbulence and turnover as officers scramble for the few jobs that are not "make-work." It is also a major cause of centralization and bureaucracy, both of which undermine combat effectiveness.

• Too often, our services follow a doctrine of attrition warfare—warfare like the battle of Verdun in World War I or the Vietnam war "body count," in which the goal is a favorable casualty exchange ratio. Instead, we need a doctrine of maneuver warfare—fighting like the Israelis or the Germans in the Blitzkrieg, where the goal is to collapse the enemy as a cohesive, effective fighting force. Maneuver warfare can bring quick victory and save lives.[4]

• In weapons, we need simplicity and numbers, not complex and often unreliable technology at such high prices that numbers are unaffordable.

• Instead of putting most of our money into fancy new weapons, we need to spend more for readiness: for training, for spare parts, for maintenance, and for ammunition for the weapons we already have.[5]

In each of these areas and many more, the military reform movement seeks to change the terms of the defense debate. It offers not just new answers, but also new questions.

The military reform movement predates cultural conservatism, but in many of the issues it raises, the reform movement is culturally conservative. It seeks to return to the traditional military culture. It wants to replace the current concern with money, budgeting, management and technology with a focus on the art of war. It calls for a return to traditional soldierly virtues instead of careerism. It turns away from the quantitative and checklist-type thinking that Secretary of Defense Robert S. McNamara emphasized and toward study of combat history and development of what Clausewitz called a "talent for judgment" in our officers. It believes the bureaucratic organizational model our services now largely follow is inappropriate for success in war, and seeks the adoption of the corporative model in its stead.

Military reform is also culturally conservative in its belief that we cannot obtain an effective defense simply by pouring more money into the military bureaucracy. Military bureaucracies behave no differently from civilian bureaucracies. They use extra resources to do more of what is comfortable internally, not what is effective in the outside, competitive world—in this case, the battlefield. Cultural conservatives find it incongruous that some other conservatives, who understand the disastrous effects of bureaucracy in other government departments, seem to overlook it when considering the military.

With other conservatives, cultural conservatives believe we need a strong defense. That means forces that can win when called upon. The last few years have shown we cannot increase our military capability very much just by spending more money. The only way we can get the defense the country needs is by coupling adequate defense spending with military reform.

Goals

• Refocus our armed services on the art of war and winning in combat, rather than budgeting, administration, and promotion politics.

• Re-establish correct defense priorities: people are most important, concepts and ideas are second, and equipment is only third.

• Reform the military promotion system to favor leaders, trainers, tacticians and strategists rather than bureaucrats, careerists, and courtiers.

• Adopt and follow a doctrine of maneuver warfare in place of reliance on attrition.

• Re-define quality in weapons to mean effectiveness in actual combat in the hands of real soldiers rather than engineering excellence under the artificial conditions of the R&D proving ground.

• Convert our armed forces from the bureaucratic to the corporative institutional model.

• Reform Congress' approach to defense, moving it away from financial micro-management toward providing long-term guidance and broad oversight.

• On the basis of genuine military reform, build an enduring, bi-partisan consensus in favor of effective armed forces as the surest guarantors of peace.

Means and Experiments

1. Make military reform a central element in the broad conservative agenda. Too often, conservatives have been followers rather than leaders in military reform, or have even opposed it. We cannot be credible in arguing for a strong defense if we propose nothing more than higher defense budgets. The public is aware that recent defense spending increases have not brought commensurate improvement in our defenses. Conservatives should make it clear that their continued support for increased defense spending is conditional on the armed services moving forward with reform. Conservative members of Congress should be encouraged to become active members of the Congressional Military Reform Caucus.

3. Reward the Army and the Marine Corps with public support for being the only services thus far to undertake their own substantive reform programs.

4. Reduce the size of the officer corps above the company grades by at least 50%. The reduction should

be accomplished by permitting early retirement rather than through a Reduction In Force (RIF) that would deprive released officers of an income and retirement benefits.

5. Eliminate the "up or out" promotion system. A competent company commander or fighter pilot who wishes to remain in his job for his entire career should be allowed to do so. As part of this reform, pay should be based more on seniority than on rank, so officers at all ranks can provide their families with a middle class standard of living.

6. Replace the current Joint Chiefs of Staff system with a National Defense Staff. A National Defense Staff would be characterized by:

  a) small size and careful selection of the most talented people;

  b) thorough education in the art of war; and

  c) permanent membership. Once an officer were designated as a National Staff Officer, his promotion would be controlled by the Staff for the remainder of his career.

7. Reorient military research and development toward production of competitive design prototypes, with the winners to be selected through actual fly-offs and shoot-offs.

8. Emphasize competition in defense procurement, with most items procured from more than one source and contracts re-bid at regular intervals.

9. Strengthen operational testing of new weapons so that it accurately reflects combat conditions and results are honestly reported.[6] No weapon should be allowed to enter production without passing rigorous operational tests.

NOTES

1. The remark was made by McNamara in an interview with Jean-Jacques Servan-Schreiber and was reported in the latter's article, "Complex Crises, Simple Solutions," in the *Washington Post,* August 30, 1987, p. C 1.

2. Three books provide useful discussions of our current military problems, although they are somewhat weak on solutions. They are:

The Straw Giant, by Arthur Hadley (New York: Random House, 1986),

To Arm a Nation: Rebuilding America's Endangered Defenses, by Richard Halloran (New York: Macmillan, 1986), and

The Pentagon and the Art of War: The Question of Military Reform, by Edward N. Luttwak (New York: Simon and Shuster, 1984).

A balanced presentation, incorporating chapters by leading reformers and defense traditionalists, is *The Defense Reform Debate,* edited by Clark, Chiarelli, McKitrick and Reed (Baltimore: Johns Hopkins University Press, 1984).

3. Here and elsewhere in this chapter, we have drawn from the official briefing of the Congressional Military Reform Caucus.

4. For a full discussion of maneuver warfare, see William S. Lind, *Maneuver Warfare Handbook* (Boulder, Co.: Westview Press, 1985).

5. For a full discussion of the reformers' recommendations, see *America Can Win: The Case for Military Reform,* by Gary Hart with William S. Lind (Bethesda, Md.: Adler and Adler, 1986).

6. In 1983, Congress accepted a Military Reform Caucus amendment to the defense authorization bill that established a strong, independent office of operational testing. Unfortunately, the Administration, which opposed the amendment, chose as director of the new office a senior employee of a major defense contractor. Under his leadership, the testing office has been neither independent nor hard-hitting.

Community Preservation
and Creation

She felt ready to go to work on the book she had set her
heart on writing: a long one, covering several generations
of life in a small midwestern city . . . she would like to
write an answer to Sinclair Lewis, whose *Main Street* had
made her so angry that after a decade she seethed when
she thought of it.

—Helen Hooven Santmyer[1]

The importance of community derives from human
nature. We all need people around us whom we know
well enough so that we can share our triumphs and
tragedies, our hopes and fears, and our day-to-day experiences with them, and they can share theirs with us.
Without such interchange, life is bleak and lonely; no
man is an island. Unless we have communities—groups
of people who spend enough time together to come to
know each other—we cannot have interchange with any
depth.

A caring community is cultural conservatives' alternative to a "throwaway/spendaway" approach to human
problems: to aborting unwanted babies, to giving the
disadvantaged an income but no help in becoming self-
supporting, to consigning the elderly to bleak nursing

126

homes. A community sees and helps people as individuals, rather than classifying them in groups and giving them "programs."

While there are many kinds of communities—professional associations, infantry squads, members of a church, etc.—the community which grows out of a stable town or neighborhood is perhaps the most important. Only this type of community offers a broad range of general, as opposed to functional relationships. In a solid community of this type, people share many things: professions, economic relationships, family ties, and simply being neighbors.

Children play a particularly important role in turning a neighborhood into a real community. Adults are drawn together by the friends their children make. Parents come to care for their neighbors' children as well as their own. Their children involve them in the nearby schools, in questions of public safety, and in cultural amenities. It is not accidental that "yuppie" neighborhoods, where most residents are single or childless couples, have difficulty forming a real community.

Communities are vital for the development and upholding of values and standards. They inculcate them in children. They encourage them in adults. And they provide social sanctions, which are far preferable to and more effective than governmental sanctions, in the event of a violation of standards.

Unfortunately, communities have been breaking down in America for at least the past thirty years. Economic changes, especially the collapse of traditional manufacturing industries and pressure on the family farm, have contributed heavily to the breakdown. So have technological changes such as the automobile and television.[2] Social policy, especially such policies as busing of schoolchildren away from neighborhood schools, have been major contributors.

Many of the causes of the breakdown of community are inherent in modern life and must be accepted. But they do not negate the need for community. That need, rooted as it is in human nature, remains as strong as ever. The challenge we face is finding ways to maintain existing communities and also to create opportunities for new communities to grow under contemporary conditions.

Of special concern is the preservation of communities that have grown up around traditional industries, generally in the Mid-Atlantic and Midwest regions. Many of these communities are still strong and viable. They have been relatively stable for three and four generations, as children followed their fathers into employment in the local factory. They are built around stable neighborhoods, strong churches and local schools, but they depend for their existence on the factory. Increasingly, the factory is in trouble, often from foreign competition. If it closes, the community dies as its younger members leave to seek employment elsewhere. Cultural conservatives are loath to see this happen, because the chances of constituting a new community under modern conditions are not high. In such cases, preservation of the economic viability of the existing community is a proper concern of government.

At the same time, we need to find ways to create new communities in the face of modernity's centrifugal tendencies. Some economic changes may assist in this, such as the ability, through new technologies, to de-centralize production. It may increasingly become possible for people to take the work to where they live, instead of having to move near the work.

Some attempts to build communities *de novo* seem to

have had some success. For example, Shaker Heights, Ohio, which was built as a planned community in the 1920s, appears to have maintained better community cohesion than have its neighboring suburbs. Such planned towns, especially if built in conjunction with new sources of employment such as industrial parks, offer at least some promise of meeting our needs.

As will inevitably be the case in relation to whole new issues, solutions are less apparent than needs. The first step towards solutions is to recognize the central need: the need each of us has to belong to some form of community. If we allow technological and other trends to prevent communities from forming or maintaining themselves, we will fuel burgeoning alienation and anomie. The need for community is part of our nature, and we must find ways to satisfy it.

Goals

• Make the need for community a national issue.
• Identify ways to assist existing communities to preserve themselves, especially in the face of dislocating economic change.
• Identify ways to assist the formation of new communities.

Means and Experiments

1. Make community preservation a major consideration in social policy. Policies such as busing that undermine communities should be looked at with strong scepticism.

2. On the local level, zoning should be encouraged, especially as a means of maintaining town centers, set-

ting minimum aesthetic standards, and channeling growth.

3. State and national encouragement of historical and architectural preservation, through such means as tax credits, are useful in preserving the specific characters of communities.

4. A Federal Community Preservation Act should be adopted, to include:

    a) State revolving funds, on the model discussed in the introduction, to enable employees of marginal industries to acquire the factory on which their community depends. The value of the factory to the local community may be far higher than to absentee owners (see economics section).

    b) State revolving funds for historic and architectural preservation.

    c) Channeling of Federal transportation funding to tie new development into existing community centers and to favor development planning that incorporates "town centers" in new developments. Mass transit lines, light rail in particular, have been used very successfully this way in Europe. On the state level, highway construction (including refusing supporting roadways to uncooperative developers) can be used the same way.

    d) Strong support for neighborhood schools.

    e) Ceding Federal taxation rights to the states for a neighborhood Police Corps program, through which a high-crime neighborhood within a larger city could obtain supplementary police (see section on crime and punishment).

    f) State revolving funds to enable long-term renters in areas undergoing redevelopment to purchase renovated homes in the same neighborhood. This could be coupled with an "urban home-steading" program that would enable poor families to purchase and renovate the house in which they are living.

g) Legislation enabling a neighborhood within a city to establish itself as a legal entity—a smaller city within a city—and to receive certain powers in the areas of crime prevention, control on development, establishment of enterprise zones, and the setting of standards for architectural quality, building maintenance, and other matters.

5. Federal agricultural support programs should be refocused to support and foster the family farm. Currently, much of the Federal funding provided under these programs goes to large agribusinesses and absentee owners. Instead, the purpose of farm support should be maintenance of rural communities built around family farms. One possible means of re-focusing these programs would be to provide support directly for farm families rather than price or other supports for certain crops. Rural enterprise zones and assistance to achieve crop diversification are also possibilities.[3]

6. Eliminate legal restrictions on work in the home. New technologies such as home computers may permit a substantial amount of work to be de-centralized, with people working in their homes instead of going to an office or factory each day. This may in turn assist community preservation, in that people can find new employment without relocating. In some cases, work in the home is currently prohibited or restricted by law, with the laws usually reflecting 19th century efforts to abolish piecework. Under current conditions, such laws prohibit what may be desirable change and should be repealed.

Notes

1. *And Ladies of the Club* (New York: G. P. Putnam's Sons, 1984), p. 1423.
2. An especially thoughtful analysis is John R. Stilgoe, *Metropolitan Corridor* (New Haven: Yale University Press, 1983).
3. See Anthony Harrigan, "What's Happening to the Southern Heartland?" *Southern Partisan,* Fall 1986/Winter 1987, pp. 24-29.

A Cultural Conservative Bill of Rights

Conservatives are generally—and properly—not enthusiastic about the fashionable habit of plucking rights out of thin air. For us, rights are idle talk outside a specific cultural and national context. Unless a nation's culture supports a right, it will have no real existence. Suddenly to postulate gay rights, animal rights, welfare rights, and so on—to act as if they could be created just by naming them—is absurd, and trivializes the concept of rights.

But there are legitimate rights: rights that have evolved in a specific culture and nation over time, usually over centuries, and that have been recognized widely. When they are violated, a wrong is committed. On this basis we have concrete American property rights, civil rights, rights to due process, etc.

All Americans also have certain cultural rights—real rights, embodied in lived experience during most of our nation's history. Because they were concretely lived and seldom violated, it was not necessary to be explicit about them in legal terms. Like all good rights, they were simply there.

Sadly, those happy days are gone, and it is time to be explicit about our cultural rights. We offer a short list here, as a sample. They are not Constitutional rights; most are informal immunities. Like all legitimate rights, there is nothing new about them. Only one is complex, because of the vast cultural importance of the subject it deals with and the confusion engendered in recent years about it: education. But there is nothing new about it, either.

As Americans we have the following cultural rights:

• We have the right to a government that recognizes traditional culture's vital role in developing and preserving a society that is both free and prosperous.

• We have the right to a government that respects traditional values and those who adhere to them—in its actions as well as its words.

• We have the right to active government support of the family as an institution essential to our culture's continuation—to the preparation and education of the next generation.

• We have the right to an education. This sounds like a small matter; it is not. It includes:

> • The right to a past of human achievement with its lessons of continuing value for the individual and the society. No human being shall be forced into a "brave new world" in which the past is forcibly obliterated or distorted, whether by Maoist Red Guards in a "cultural revolution" or by university professors who replace education with indoctrination and ideology.

> • Each generation has the right to the classics of its culture, without censorship or bowdlerization imposed by passing ideological movements, left or right.

> • Each generation has the right to be equipped with skills and understanding sufficient to read and grasp the classics of its culture.

> • Each generation has a right to receive its total

cultural inheritance in such a way that it can review the work of the previous generation. Each generation has a right to find more of value in its past, and to make better use of its past, than did the previous generation.

- We have a right to a government that understands what education is and why it is important: that it is the only means by which the culture can continue itself generation after generation. Government must understand that this, and nothing less, is the goal and focus of education.

- Within this concept of education, we all have the right to guide our children's instruction, including the right to send them to schools that teach values, without suffering financial or other punishments. In general, education is more likely to perform its cultural duties when it is controlled by parents than when it is directed by a central state apparatus.

- We have the right to effective protection against crime. A government that leaves its citizens' persons and property to be frequent victims of violent crime loses its legitimacy. Government owes its citizens sufficient protection so that they can live free of fear of violent crime.

- We have the right not to be confronted with pornography.

- We have the right to assistance in the preservation of our communities, especially when they are threatened with dissolution or destruction.

Unfinished Business

To this point, we have offered an agenda. We have identified problems, then translated them into policy goals and possible means to achieve the goals. It is not a complete or finished agenda. In coming months, we will be working to expand and develop it. We need and will welcome assistance in that task, including from people who may previously have seen conservatives as opponents.

But if we are to come to grips with the roots of our current national decline, we also need to look beyond issues that fit neatly into an agenda. Many disturbing cultural changes cannot be shoehorned into a problem/goals/solutions framework, at least at this stage. Yet we need to identify and think about them. They include:

• *What might be called the moral climate: not only the values, but the attitude toward the concept of values, that prevail among us.* Too often, values seem to have yielded their place and function to fashion. Do we want a culture in which fashion is the philosopher's stone, the ultimate criterion by which ideas and actions are judged? Most of us would answer no, yet it seems that is what we are coming to.

It is all too evident in the life-styles of our elites. When we look at many of them, we see only fashion. The prevailing standard is set not in terms of living up to sound values, but in BMWs or Mercedes, career advancement, lines of credit, of being seen in the "right" places with the "right" people so as to show access and power. Status and fashion are the only merits, and Hollywood, rather than Jerusalem, Athens, or Rome, is the source of standards.

Political issues themselves are increasingly a matter of fashion, of what Tom Wolfe calls "radical chic." During the Vietnam War, it was fashionable to believe that the North Vietnamese were kindly agrarian reformers who sought nothing but a peaceful pluralism for their South Vietnamese cousins. The belief was demonstrably absurd, but it was powerful because it was fashionable. When, after 1975, the true nature of communist intentions for South Vietnam became obvious to all, why was there little outcry from those who had championed the Northern cause? Because Vietnam was no longer a fashionable issue.

Traditionally, a moral climate wherein fashion is the highest good would have been opposed vigorously by moral leaders, by academics, churchmen, and men of letters. Yet here too the moral climate is unhealthy. Too often, it reflects a cultural death-wish, a desire not to mend and restore Western culture but to bring it crashing down. The very people who should be most aware of the West's great achievement, of its creation of societies uniquely free and prosperous, are its greatest detractors, turning instead to narrow ideologies that have strewn our century with the bodies of the innocent. And this too is fashion: the fashion of the academic set.

None of this is accidental: it is a logical result of our society's rewards and punishments. We admire and reward the man of fashion, and look upon the moral man as, at best, a sad drudge. If the morality is sufficiently bizarre, it too can be fashionable, at least for a while. But what earlier times would have called the solid citizen, the person who advocates and follows traditional values, is looked on as a figure of fun, an appropriate butt of jokes and comedy. If he lies down and takes it, more is heaped upon him. If he fights back, he is portrayed as a dangerous bluenose, someone who would bring back the lynch mob and let police into our bedrooms. Meanwhile, those who "go along to get along," who have no values beyond what is popular, are held up as models and rewarded with great riches.

How do we change the moral climate?

• *A culture at war with itself, in which the brain and the body are pitted against each other.* Prior to the late 17th century, the Western intellectual's accepted function was to develop and defend society's core belief: Christianity. This was metaphysics, the discipline of explaining all phenomena on the basis of reconciled reason and revelation. The intellectual held the same basic world view as the peasant, the soldier, the officeholder, the townsman and, of course, the churchman. All were part of a coherent, symbiotic whole.

The Enlightenment changed all this. Following the lead of Locke, among others, intellectuals threw over metaphysics for a science based exclusively on sensory perception. Revelation went out the window, not all at once, but by the late 18th century not much was left of it beyond ritual bows. The Enlightenment gave the intellectuals a new role. Instead of being the defenders of society's core beliefs, they were to be its critics, its attackers, change agents to whom the beliefs of most of their fellow men were "obscurantism," which they had as their new duty to replace with the light of pure reason.

And so our cultural civil war began. It continues today, because the bulk of non-elite society—the "silent majority"—continues to adhere in large measure to traditional values and ways of living, which grew out of Christianity. In many cases the religion itself is gone or reduced to a formality, but its values and the habits it built remain.

So we continue at war with ourselves, intellectuals and the elite they influence following one code, the body of society, its "workers and peasants," another. The price is high for both combatants. The intellectuals often feel alienated, as indeed they are, from most of their fellow citizens. They regard them as the great "booboisie," and they are in turn regarded as "pointy headed intellectuals." The mass of society has few coherent spokesmen for its beliefs, and feels itself assailed by the hostile elite culture. Each retreats further into its own world: the intelligentsia into the campuses, the major media, and government, the silent majority into its churches, its bars and the NRA.

How do we end our cultural civil war and make peace between society's body and brain?

• *An increasingly defective elite.* Educated by an intelligentsia hostile to the society it inhabits and often left with little more than fashion as a core value, our elite no longer performs its functions. It no longer provides leadership, sets and enforces high standards, subordinates short-term pressures to long-term goals, provides sound policy, or serves the society of which it is a part. More and more, it is a yuppie elite, whose life revolves around materialism and status. Its mottos are "You are what you own" and "I'm out to get mine."

One effect of the decay of the elite—which as late as the immediate post-World War II period was largely still a service elite—is a change in the nature of ambition. Traditionally, especially in America, it was an ambition to do something. Among the East-coast, Ivy League elite, it was often an ambition to serve the government in such positions as the foreign service. Among the commercial elite, it was an ambition to build or make something. We certainly had our new rich, those whose ambition was money or status, but they were not looked upon as models. Boston held its nose at Newport.

Now, the elite's ambition is to be something: to sit in a prestigious office, to become CEO or make partner, to drive a Mercedes and be seen as wealthy and successful. Success is defined as moving up the career ladder, and everything is subordinate to that—including producing a sound product. An example of the change is the use of the word "professional." Once it meant a standard to which work was done. Now it is a description of status.

Another change—a fundamental cultural change—proceeding from the defective elite is a change in group dynamics. Traditionally, when Americans formed a working group, the automatic focus was on the product. If necessary, people within the group were prepared to create friction with other members in order to produce a sound product. Today, increasingly, the focus of each group member is not the product but building personally useful relationships with other group members—finding patrons and clients and "networking" them. If the product must be sacrificed in order to please potential patrons, that is not a major concern.

Our elite is failing in its function. The evidence is our growing inability to compete successfully with other nations. More and more people recognize this failure. What few yet recognize is that the functional failure is due to a failure in standards, morals and culture among the elite. It is defective in its competence because it is defective in its culture.

How do we repair or replace our defective elite?

• *Media*. One of our proudest national traditions, enshrined in our Constitution, is freedom of the press. It is closely related to another of our basic freedoms, freedom of speech. Our Founding Fathers believed a free press vital, because it was essential to an informed citizenry, on which democracy depends.

However, the nature of the media has altered greatly from what the Founding Fathers envisioned. Instead of being a mirror of events, the media have become creators and shapers of events. An event or an issue that does not receive media (especially television) coverage does not exist. As early as the 1930s, radio could make real a wholly fictitious event, as it dramatically demonstrated in the broadcast of H. G. Wells' *The War of the Worlds*. Today, television determines reality, not only in its news reports but equally in its programming. *Dallas* is quite real in many American homes. At the same time, the family that follows traditional values has become unreal because it is seldom portrayed on television. Such a family finds that the media, which is now a part of the surrounding community, no longer reflects or reinforces its values.

Nor does the power of the media stop with the content of its programming. The question is not merely one of the effect on our lives of the favorable portrayal of violence and extra-marital sex, of confusion of outward appearance and inward worth, of brilliant children set against obtuse parents, of such satires of the traditional family as the Archie Bunker show, and of the almost universal television message that material wealth and status are properly the highest goals. The whole mode of transmission of television, in which the viewer is passive, his mind inert, has tremendous effects. So does the level of thought and language represented on television. So does the very small content of a half-hour news broadcast, in terms of the number of words the time can accommodate, compared to a newspaper or magazine article. So does the fact that certain images and styles "work" on television while others, which may have much greater depth or value, do not.

The Founding Fathers did not envision that freedom of the press would lead to a culture largely shaped and determined by the media—media which answer to no authority beyond commercial success.

This substantial change in the media's power and role compels us to confront some difficult questions:

• To what extent do media themes and portrayals alter people's expectations, despite their conscious knowledge that the material is fictional?

• To what extent does a steady diet of dramatic solutions, achieved within an hour's time, lessen a people's ability to grapple with complex problems?

• To what extent do heroes who are passionately involved and caring drifters, or children with prodigious sagacity, or incorruptible sybarites, or some other sort of social miracle becloud people's understanding of the nature of real life?

• Is it safe to assume that the levels of literacy, education, speech, and ability to think logically required by an advanced society will be produced by a culture dominated by media programmed to fit the lowest common denominator?

• What will be the sensitivity to real heroism, tragedy, achievement or need in people to whom everything, even the newest brand of soapflakes, is presented at a fever-pitch of intensity? Is the current fascination with horror, violence and gore in part a product of the fact that, with everything intensely "hyped," nothing less than flowing blood makes any impression at all?

• What is the meaning of television's transition from defining sensual pleasure, through the way its characters live, to providing it directly through such means as rock videos?

• Can we leave a force with such power responsible only to itself, subject only to such criticism as it accepts and therefore broadcasts? If not, to what should it be made answerable?

These questions invite thoughtful attention from all parts of the political spectrum. They are worrisome because we do not know the answers to them, yet we dare not risk being wrong. It is clear that a very powerful cultural force is loose, free and almost wholly unrestrained, and we do not know where it is propelling us. We also do not know how we might restrain it without putting freedom of the press and freedom of speech at risk, which cultural conservatives certainly do not want to do.

• *Aesthetics*. Aesthetics is so difficult a subject, as a matter for public policy or even public discussion, that we habitually leave it aside. In doing so, we imply that it does not matter.

Yet aesthetics does matter. It matters very greatly to our quality of life. There is no better example than architecture. The International Style has done great damage to our urban environments, converting many of them into cold, forbidding, unlivable canyons of steel and glass. We now see a long overdue turn away from the International Style, a turn toward smaller scale, warm materials, ornamentation, and—as a comment on the current state of architecture—toward architectural preservation. This turn is itself evidence that aesthetics matters.

How do we begin a sensible public discussion of aesthetics?

• *The direction and pace of change.* It is a truism that change is modernity's one constant—rapid change. No one argues that we can or should stop it. But can we not raise some questions about both its direction and its pace?

The question of direction of change can be asked simply: have things changed in such a way over the last 30 years that today's America is better—a more satisfactory place to live—than the America of 1957? In certain ways it certainly is. Our medicine is more advanced, racial discrimination is gone from our laws, and the level of our technology is incomparably higher.

But are we, on the whole, better satisfied? For every area of real progress, we can see several negative counterparts. Over the last thirty years, the rates of crime and drug use have grown appallingly, our public schools have deteriorated, our families have weakened, and for many of us, our job satisfaction and security have lessened. The overall trend seems negative—a trend of decay, with some exceptions, rather than a trend of progress with occasional failures.

Even our areas of progress have their dark sides. No one would deny our progress in civil rights. But is the black community better off on the whole than it was three decades ago? Have we not resolved one of its problems only to fall into others, most prominently the growth of a black underclass?

Are we seeing signs, at least in some areas, that we are beyond the peak of the curve in change—that we get relatively few new benefits from each large increment of investment? This happens in almost every field at some point, and when it does, it points to a need for some basic changes in direction.

The pace of change is also a concern. It is so rapid that generations live in different worlds, and even within a single generation, people are afflicted with a sense of rootlessness, of anomie. Many observers suggest this is unavoidable, because the pace of change is driven by changing technology. To slow it, we would have to adopt the prescription of the Spanish Carlists: rip up the railroads and bring back the Inquisition.

But how much of the change we have seen since 1957 has really been driven by technology? Obviously, some has; in 1957, the Soviet Union did not have the technology to deliver thousands of nuclear warheads on American soil, and today it does. But are we ascribing to technology some change which has in fact been driven by culture? If so, we may have at least some control over the pace of change, because cultural change is not always driven by what happens in laboratories. If, for example, we do not like the results of the change to families where both parents work, we can move to restore the family wage—itself originally a product of a 19th century reform movement.

We need to think about both the direction and the pace of change. Neither is wholly ordered by some cosmic engine we can neither see nor control. Here, as elsewhere, man can at least influence his own destiny. One of this nation's traditional cultural strengths has been its belief that it can shape its own destiny. Perhaps it is time to apply that belief to thinking about change itself.

Where do we go from here? As we have said repeatedly through this document, the ideas we have offered here are only a beginning. Large policy areas, such as drug abuse, public health, judicial reform, and the role of the elderly in our society have yet to be addressed. The completion of a new national agenda, one based on culture rather than economics, one that reflects the fundamental cultural conservative insight that traditional culture is functional culture, must draw on far more talent than we can offer.

But we can and do offer a beginning, and a challenge. The challenge is writ large: it is nothing less than the restoration of our national greatness. We can again be the world's leader in the competitiveness of our products, the excellence of our education, the strength of our families, the civic order in our cities, the effectiveness of our armed forces, in all the many ways which made America a beacon of hope for all the peoples of this earth. We can do all of this and more, if we will remember what our forefathers knew so well: that America was great because its people were good.

On this truth depends our future as a people and a nation.

INSTITUTE FOR CULTURAL CONSERVATISM

WILLIAM S. LIND
DIRECTOR

William Sturgiss Lind is a native of Cleveland, Ohio, born July 9, 1947. He graduated from Dartmouth College in 1969 and received a Masters from Princeton University in 1971.

From 1973 through 1976, Mr. Lind served as a legislative aide to Senator Robert Taft, Jr., specializing in defense. He held a similar position with Senator Gary Hart from 1977 through 1986. In addition to serving as director of the Institute of Cultural Conservatism at the Free Congress Foundation, Mr. Lind is president of the Military Reform Institute and an advisor to Representative Denny Smith (R-OR).

Mr. Lind is author of the *Maneuver Warfare Handbook* and co-author, with Gary Hart, of *America Can Win: The Case for Military Reform*. He has written numerous articles for professional journals including the *Marine Corps Gazette*, *Air University Review*, and *The Naval Institute Proceedings*. He is a frequent lecturer at Air Force Squadron Officer School, the Army and Air War Colleges, and the National Defense University.

WILLIAM H. MARSHNER
SENIOR SCHOLAR

Professor of Theology at Christendom College in Front Royal, Virginia, Mr. Marshner pursued his graduate studies at Yale as a Woodrow Wilson fellow and at the University of Dallas as a Weaver fellow. He is a frequent contributor to scholarly journals and a prominent lecturer in theology, philosophy, and politics. He belongs to the American Catholic Philosophical Association and has served as president of the Mariological Society of America. His monographs include *The New Creatures and the New Politics*, a defense of Christian political activism, and *The Morality of Political Action*.